ITALIAN BOYS
at Fort Missoula, Montana
1941-1943

ITALIAN BOYS
at Fort Missoula, Montana
1941-1943
by Umberto Benedetti

Copyright @ 1991 by Umberto Benedetti
All Rights Reserved

No part of this book may be reproduced in any form or by any means, electronic or mechanical, including photocopying, recording, or by any information storage and retrieval system, without prior permission in writing from the author, except in the case of brief quotations embodied in critical articles and reviews.

Library of Congress Card Catalog Number 91-92245
ISBN 1-57510-035-5

First Printing: November 1997

Books Published:
    Montana-Noon, A Very Bright Day, Friends (1985)
    Translated two reports for the State Department about Bears, written in Italian (1985)
    The Lifestyle of Italian Internees at Fort Missoula: Montana - Bella Vista (1986)
    The Lady and Her Lover (1987)
    A Cultural Freedom of the Press (1988)
    Histonium - a small brochure telling the story of the birth of Italy (1989)

For information, write: Umberto Benedetti
610 East Broadway, #3
Missoula, Montana 59802
(406) 549-7735

Published for Umberto Benedetti by

Pictorial Histories Publishing Co., Inc.
Missoula, Montana 59801

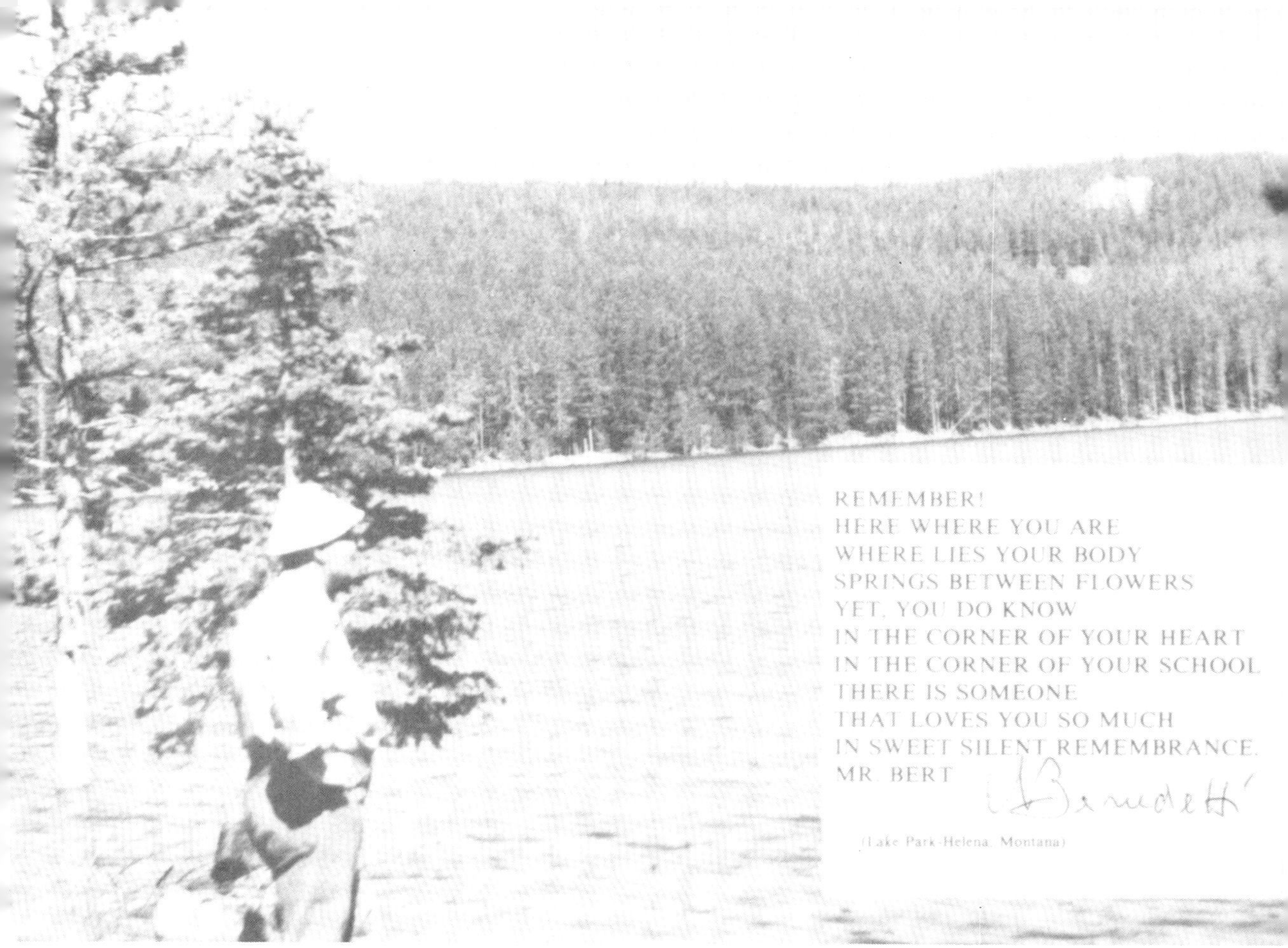

REMEMBER!
HERE WHERE YOU ARE
WHERE LIES YOUR BODY
SPRINGS BETWEEN FLOWERS
YET, YOU DO KNOW
IN THE CORNER OF YOUR HEART
IN THE CORNER OF YOUR SCHOOL
THERE IS SOMEONE
THAT LOVES YOU SO MUCH
IN SWEET SILENT REMEMBRANCE.
MR. BERT

(Lake Park-Helena, Montana)

Dedicated to Fort Missoula,
my first home, 1941-1943

Introduction

This is the second edition of the Fort Missoula Internment Camp book. This edition contains some pictures that have never before been published.

I changed the title of the book to *Italian Boys at Fort Missoula, Montana* to give to the reader a different point of view of that turbulent time in the 1940s. The first edition was called "Che Bella Vista," which means "what a beautiful sight." Nonetheless, in the common Italian language, many other variations can be given. Missoula was a beautiful place for the sailors coming from the two oceans bordering the United States. The citizens of Missoula may not have appreciated how wonderful the panorama surrounding them was then. Now, the Missoula Valley has been transformed into a community that is in danger of losing the beauty of Nature.

Contrary to some public opinions, Fort Missoula was a relocation camp for Italians coming from all parts of California, including Hollywood. Most were civilians, but some were ideologic Fascists who were interned temporarily while awaiting new orders coming from Washington, D.C. or from California Immigration Services.

The Fort Missoula camp was the best of all camps in the United States, and was a model because the Italians organized themselves in such a way that the citizens of Missoula came often to see all the activities and theatrical performances that we had. As far as I can remember, the Japanese had few activities in comparison, because the Italians came from the theatrical ship *Il Conte Biancamano*. Contrary to some public opinion, the Japanese were treated as gentlemen, just like the Italians or any other people coming from outside the camp.

The Immigration guards were very friendly with everyone, considering that the United States was fully engaged in World War II. However, it was their duty to check everyone, as a regulation of the camp. Even for someone with a good command of the English language, it would have been difficult to escape and reach New York, California, or Chicago. At that time there was not even a good road to reach those distances and it was a risky idea. On the other hand, no one really wanted to escape because they were treated very well by the people of Missoula.

History is a chronological record of significant events.

Events, are the subject of this story.

It is my purpose to focus on that turbulent period of time in the early 1940s when I was interned at the Alien Detention Camp at Fort Missoula, and with photographs and documents to tell my story as accurately as possible. This book chronicles some events that are told here for the first time.

> "History is what today will be tomorrow."
> —Tibus 42 B.C.

Umberto Benedetti

Acknowledgments

My appreciation goes to Ms. Pamela Cobb, who with great patience helped me with typing this work.

I thank the following persons, who shared with me the photographs and documents included in this book:

    Visciano Raimondo, Florida
    Inga Paollilo, New York
    Agostini Ronzitti, New York
    Vincent Rivieccio, California
    Mary Ann Apice Filiberto, California
    Bill Sharp, Missoula, Montana
    John C. Moe, Lolo, Montana
    Gregory Marmorato, Missoula, Montana
    Carole Incoronato Toppins, Missoula, Montana
    Professor Carol Van Valkenburg for her suggestions, Missoula, Montana

Table of Contents

Remembering the Past 1
Entrance to Fort Missoula 2
Fort Missoula Recreation Center Hall 12
Mr. John C. Moe—A Reflection of the Past 13
Joy of Living in Montana 24
Fort Missoula Internment Camp 27
Adjustment Within the Camp 35
Sturdy Boats Built for the Rivers 36
Theme 40
Alfredo Cipolato 41
Tools of the Trade 44
Documentation of Immigration 49
Remembering the Trips 54
Historical Museum at Fort Missoula 63
Raymond Visciano 65
To the Readers 67
Capt. Paolo Stefano Saglietto 85
John Battista Paolillo 86
Donato Giuseppe Incoronato 90
Power of Labor Man 99
Vincent Rivieccio Collection 103
About the Author 125
Index 127

Remembering the Past

During World War II, Fort Missoula became a detention center for Italian and some Japanese civilians. Here are some bits of the stories as I remember them. With war threatening, many Americans in 1941 feared that some German and Italian civilians living in or entering the United States might prove to be enemy spies or saboteurs. As part of President Roosevelt's decision to get tough with the European Axis powers (Germany, Italy, and their allies), the United States began seizing Axis merchant ships in American waters (including *Il Conte Biancamano*, which was in the Panama Canal) and detaining the crews. Deporting all these men became impossible as international relations worsened. The Immigration and Naturalization Service detained the aliens first at Ellis Island, and then at internment camps until they could be deported or released.

The internment center at Fort Missoula was just one of several throughout the United States. Missoula was a logical choice for such a center because of its remote location. However, before the Italians moved to the Fort, a group of officers from *Il Conte Biancamano*, together with Immigration personnel, came to Missoula not only for its location but for the climate and the environment of its location.

The first group of Italian internees from Ellis Island, New York, began to arrive in Missoula in the spring of 1941. They lived in the existing buildings until they could complete the camp with dormitories, fences and other structures. During that time, the center consisted of dormitories, a mess hall, laundry, tailor shop, post office, shoe shop, carpenter shop, blacksmith shop, and a recreation area. Originally designed to hold 3,000 internees, no more than half that number were ever in Missoula at one time.

After Pearl Harbor, the government also transferred Japanese-Americans to Missoula, eventually separating them from the Italians. By April 1944, all of the civilian internees were released and allowed to return to their homes.

By far the largest ethnic group of internees at Fort Missoula were the Italians. On May 18, 1941, 1,200 Italian merchant seamen and civilians arrived at the Fort. They called the center Che Bella Vista (beautiful view) and were put to work constructing the rest of the camp.

Accommodations at Fort Missoula far exceeded the guidelines set down by the Geneva Convention. Food rationing did not apply to the internees. Although the center was patrolled by armed guards, heavy security measures proved to be unnecessary—no one was ever missing. Guards claimed that Boy Scouts could keep the Italians in! The guards' main problem was keeping curious Missoulians out.

Although the valley had beautiful scenery, boredom became a legitimate complaint. As wartime tensions relaxed and the shortage of men in the Missoula work force became acute, officials allowed some Italian internees to work in town. They were employed as chefs, waiters, busboys, and room cleaners at both the Palace and Florence Hotels, and worked as orderlies in Missoula's hospitals. Italian work crews also helped in the sugar beet harvest.

Working on a day-to-day basis, the internees were accepted by the community. Missoulians greatly appreciated their work and some internees made Missoula, as well as Montana, their home.

The Entrance to Fort Missoula

The original entrance to Fort Missoula in the 1940s was very romantic-looking, presenting an enviable open-space view to the human eye. In those days, a musician/artist/writer from Hollywood was so impressed with the view that he wrote a piece of music compared to Wolfgang Amadeus Mozart, when he traveled by carriage through the forest along that beautiful road.

The entrance to Fort Missoula inspired more than one artist in the camp. The stretch of entrance was lined with a green column of trees on both sides of the road, and impressed upon the 1,200 sailors that the camp was not a concentration camp, but rather a romantic entrance to a place that they would stay to see the blue sky rather than the blue, lonely sea. The only exception was that they would be counted every morning.

The first group of Italian internees to view this beautiful vista created a new name for Fort Missoula—"Che Bella Vista," or "what a beautiful sight." It also means the best place they ever saw. The adjectives can be translated in so many common words that there will be no end to it. Although the internees were within a wire fence, they enjoyed the peaceful calmness of that place, coming from the open sea. They came from a warm temperature to a dry cold so that even in June some were shivering.

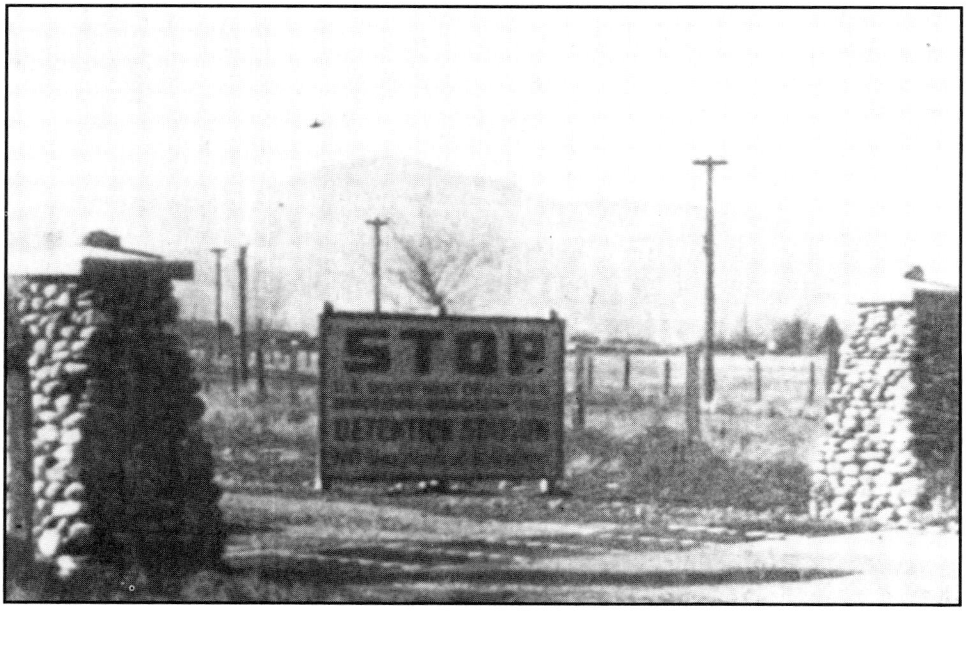
STOP

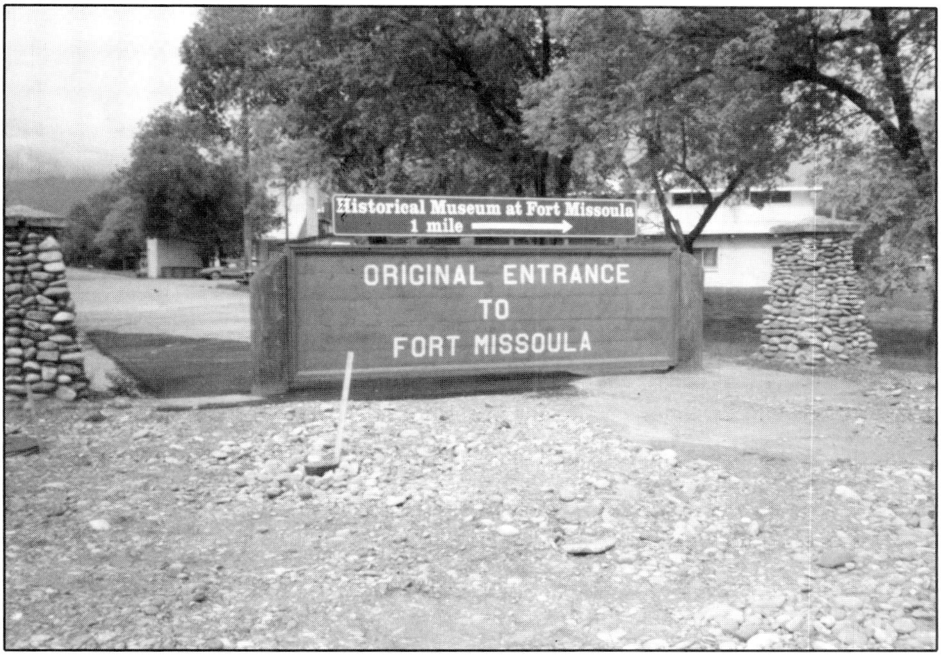
Historical Museum at Fort Missoula
1 mile
ORIGINAL ENTRANCE
TO
FORT MISSOULA

This was the original entrance to Fort Missoula which is now closed to through traffic.

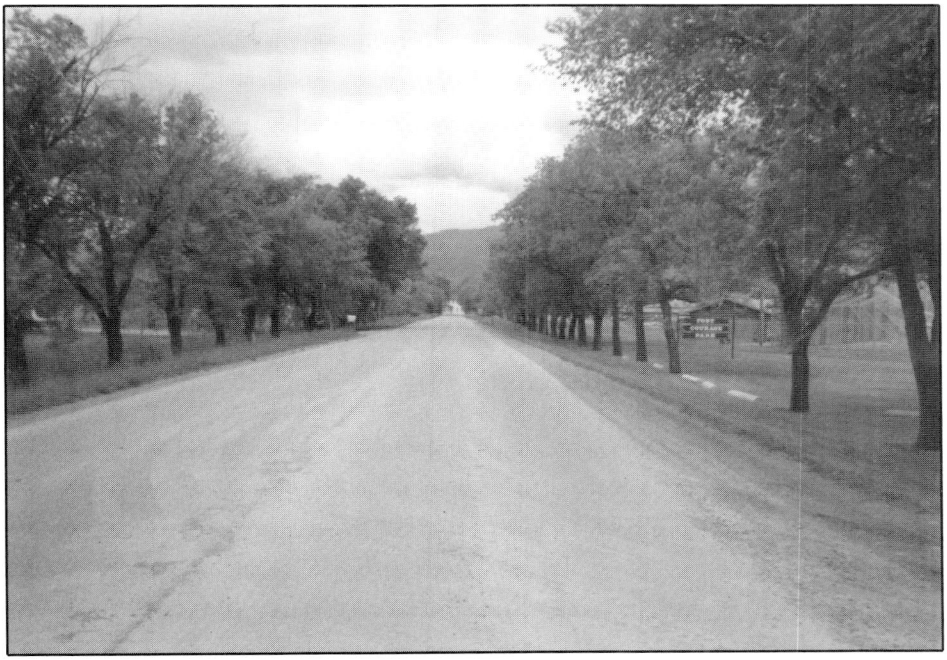

The entrance road to the Fort.

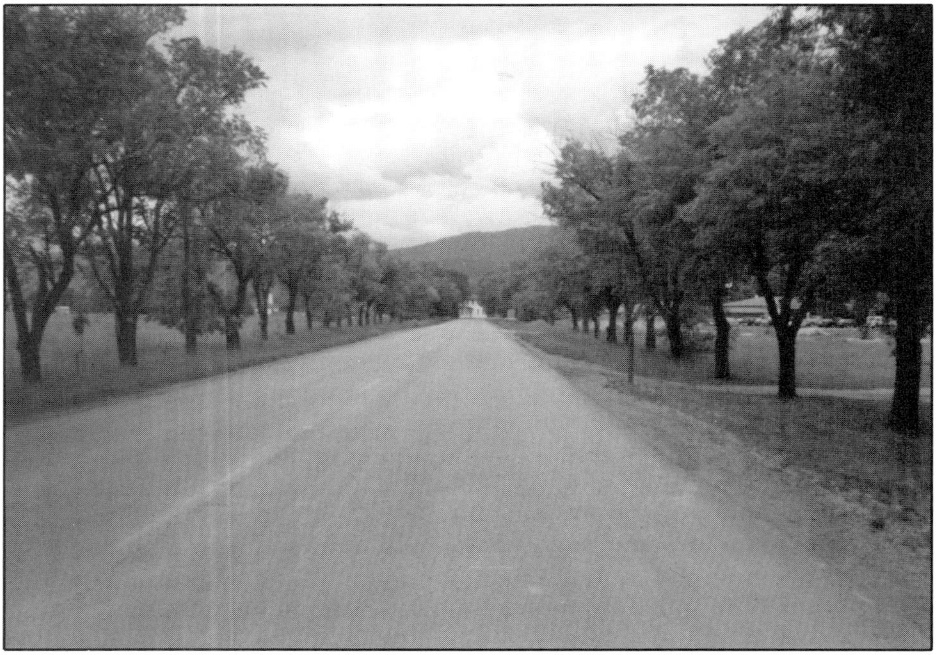

The entrance road to the Fort.

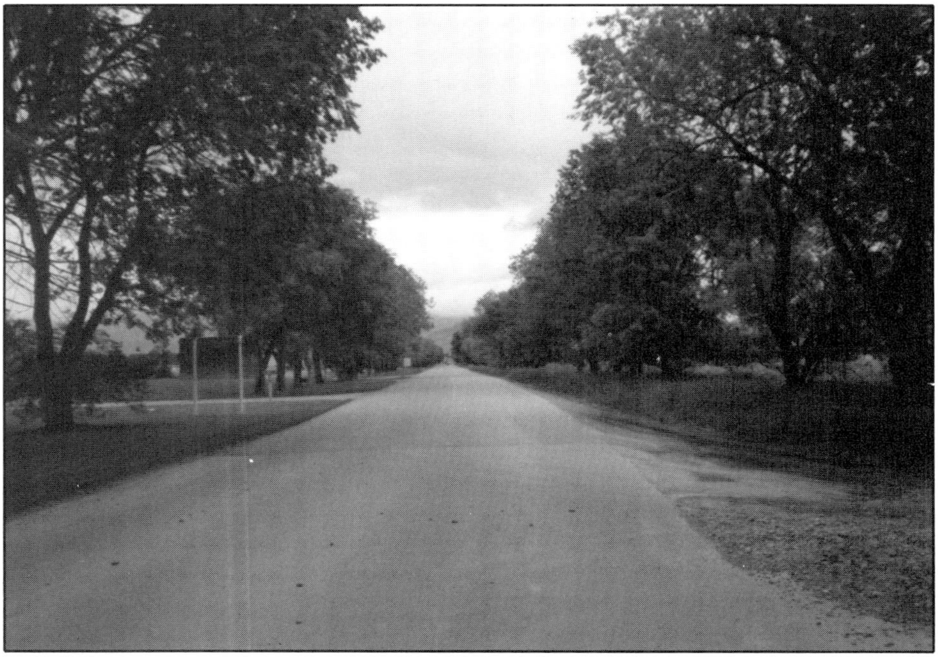

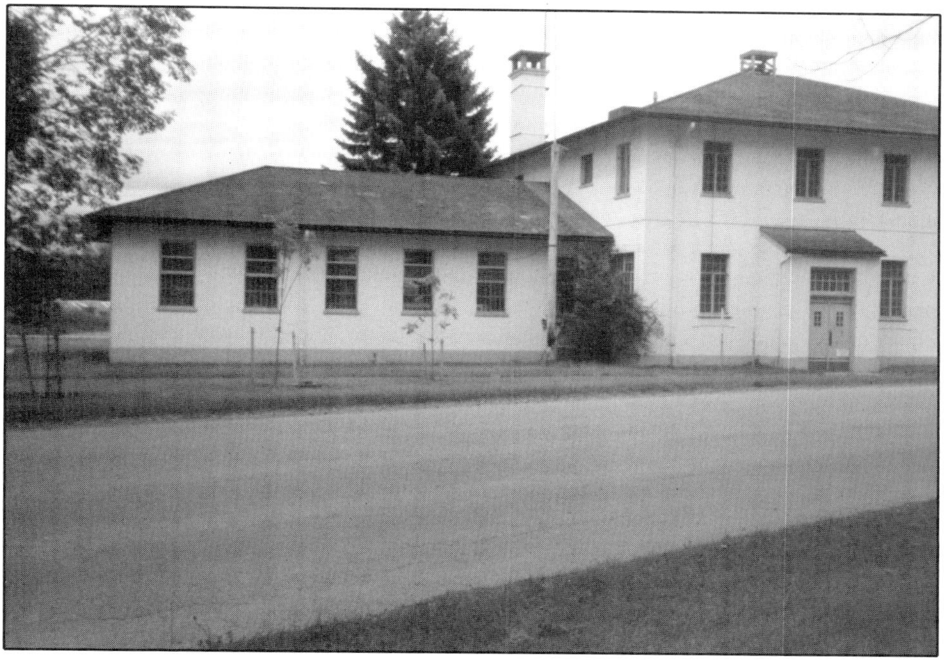

Original Fort Fire Station.

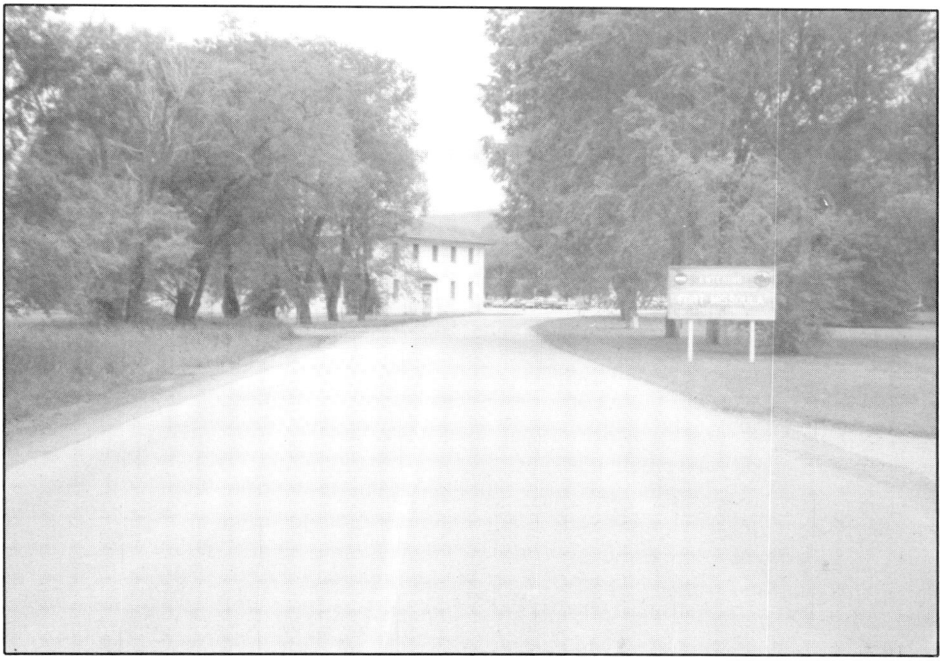

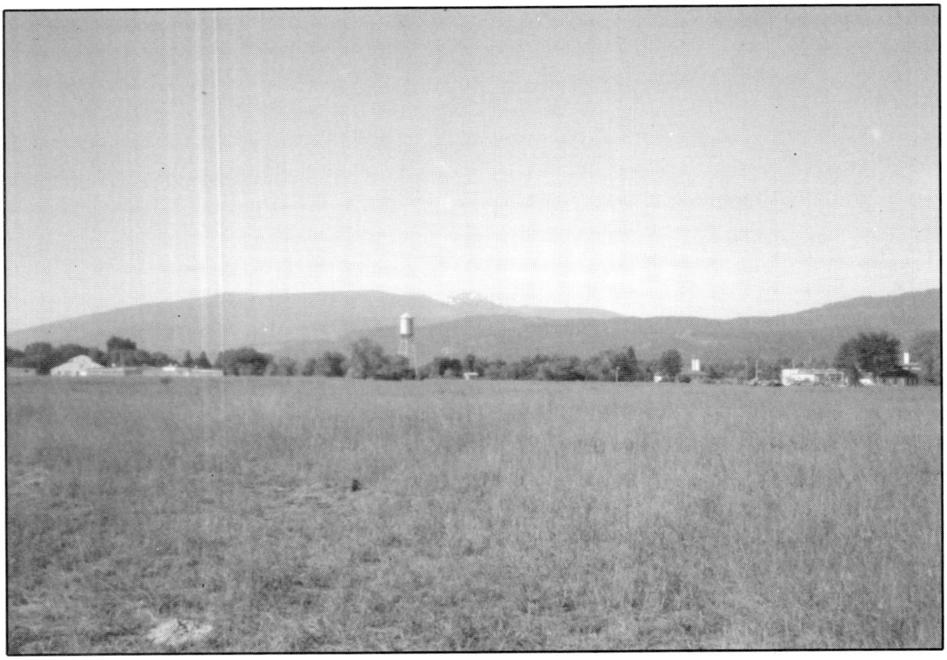

View of the Fort looking south.

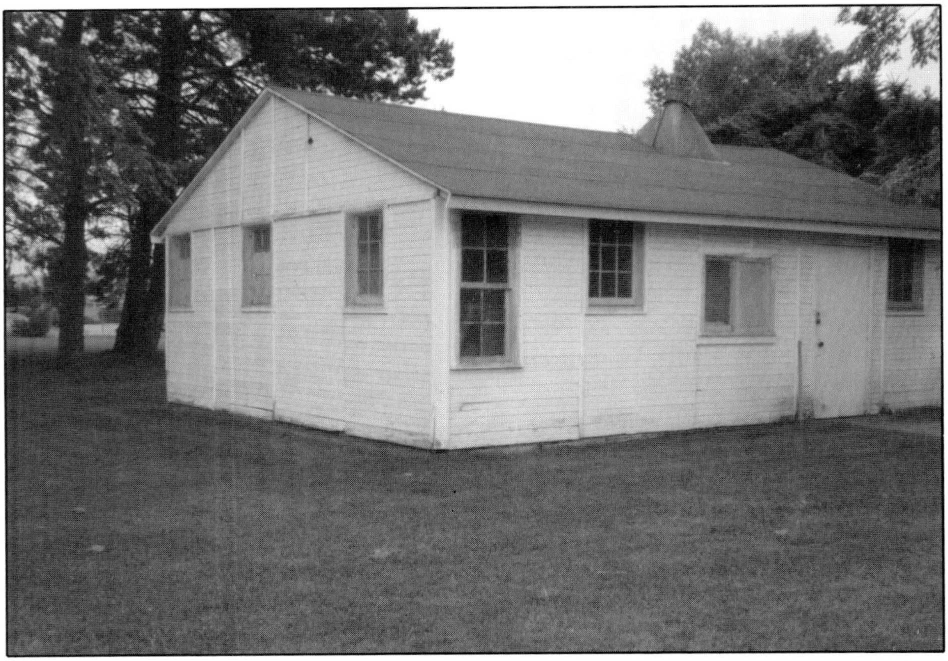

One of the original camp barracks has been reconstructed on the grounds of the Historical Museum at Fort Missoula.

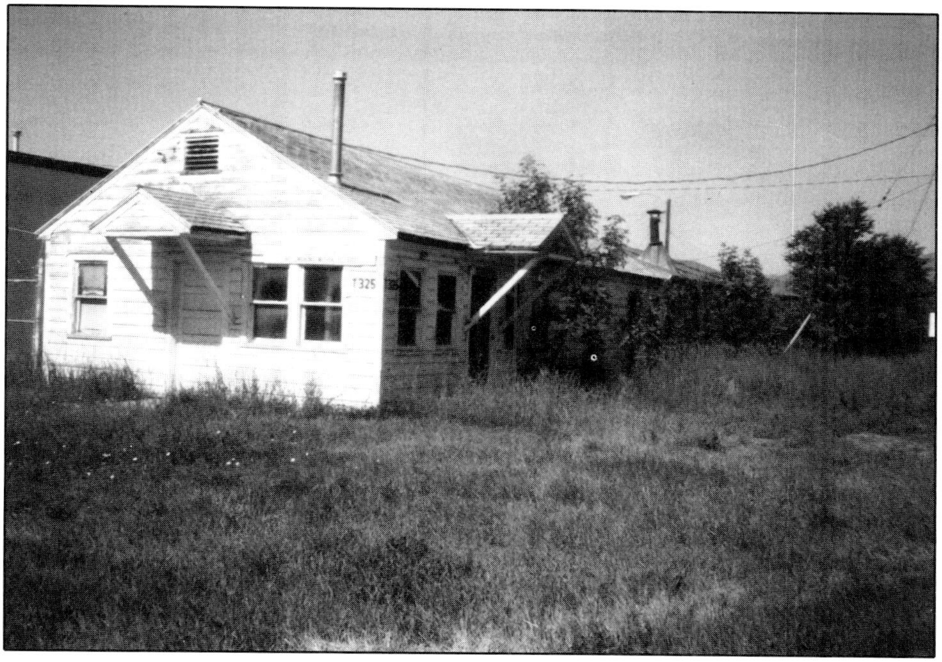
T325

Inside the above barracks was written "Italia Bella"—"beautiful Italy." That was in 1941-1943, when some young boy of 17 or 19 still had the feeling of his homeland.

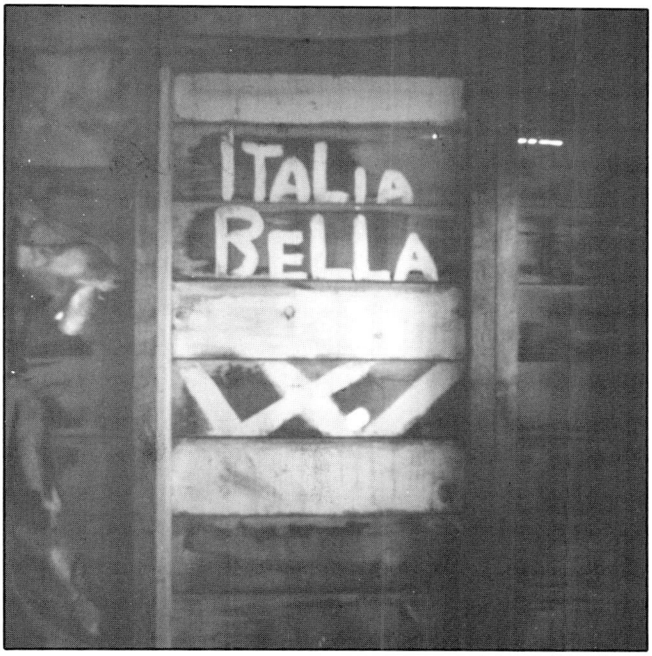
ITALIA
BELLA

La Lanterna Di Genova—The Genoa Lighthouse

This lighthouse is well-known throughout the world. Its special characteristic, as a certain poet said, is that "It seems that a star is moving itself," and serves as a faithful guide to seamen. Erected on rocks, it is 1,315 feet high and from the top is a panorama that can hardly be described, a view unrivaled in its beauty. The internees at Fort Missoula built a replica and a garden, although they do not exist anymore. This lighthouse could have been a tourist attraction for the Fort.

The Detention Camp at Fort Missoula, 1941-1943

1. These two pages tell about the rules, regulations and practices that were adopted within the camp for internees at Fort Missoula, approved by Mr. N.D. Collaer for the U.S. Immigration and Naturalization Service, with the cooperation of Mr. Alessandro De Luca, Mayor and Commissioner of the Camp.

2. For the crews of "Il Conte Biancamano, Arsa, Aussa, Alberta, Brennero, San Leonardo," the rules were equal for everyone, without distinction.

3. It was absolutely prohibited to pass over the wire fence. A person had to have a special pass in order to go outside the camp.

4. The internees had to come outside to be counted in the morning, as well as in the evening.

5. The officers' supervisor, in cooperation with the non-commissioned officers, took turns at the 6:00 a.m. wakeup trumpet call. The internees had to come out without delay, because they had to take care of beds and other items until 9:30 a.m. Then each supervisor had to inspect their respective apartment sections to see if they were in order.

6. In each section of the building, the internees had a deposit of footlockers. The rooms were opened from 9:30 to 10:30 in the morning, and from 3:00 to 4:00 in the afternoon.

7. Everyone cooperated during cleaning and maintenance.

8. In the morning, each internee had to go to the washroom in order to avoid confusion and to be in time for breakfast.

9. Each person was responsible for their personal hygiene and had to keep the washroom, toilets and shower in good condition.

10. Each person assisted in cleaning the camp when necessary.

11. Everyone was responsible for keeping in good condition all the materials that belonged to the camp.

12. Often, supervisors from the U.S. Department of Justice inspected the camp along with the camp officers.

13. To the right of the building was the space reserved for soccer and other athletic activities.

14. The internees had to walk on the sidewalks and not on the lawns.

15. The internees were advised of the availability of medical services.

16. On all holidays there was a Mass at 9:30 in the Section C building at the camp.

17. There were two barber shops at the camp.

18. There was a shop that sold stamps, cigarettes, and other items. The shop was open from 9:00 a.m. until 6:00 p.m.

19. There was a mailbox, and the mail came at 10 a.m. The letters had to be addressed carefully so that they would not be returned but would go to Italy.

20. In the Section C building, there was a deposit of linens. Linens were changed every week during the work hours between 8:00 a.m. and 3:00 p.m.

21. If someone wanted to buy an item from downtown Missoula, he had to ask an officer, or sometimes was allowed to go with the officer to buy the item.

22. The U.S. government supplied all food and some clothing.

23. Mail call and other group meetings were called by the trumpeter.

Translated by the author.

FORT MISSOULA RECREATION CENTER

"Built during the year of 1939"
Official opening - February 22, 1940

Architect - Robert Reamer : (from a Seattle Firm; Specialty Logs :)
    * Reamer built the Old Faithful Inn - opening for the 1904 season , Also designed many other log buildings.

Builder - W.P.A. (WORKS PROGRESS ADMINISTRATION)-U.S. Government :

Logs - from the Civilian Conservation Corps
    ' mostly of lodgepole pine which was cut , peeled and shaped at the Post & Pole Yard of the CCC Co. 1963 , Squaw Creek CCC Camp on the Gallatin National Forest .
    - Shipped on the Milwaukee Railroad from Gallatin Gateway-

<u>Grand Opening</u> : February 22, 1940 , with the Fort Missoula CCC District Boxing "Golden Gloves Tournament"

Fort Missoula Recreation Center Premier Tonight
FEBRUARY 22, 1940.

This new improvement at Fort Missoula is to be the scene of the Golden Gloves district championship boxing contests starting tonight. Besides the main room on the first floor containing the ring, it has bowling alleys and other sports opportunities to make it a center of attraction at the fort. A kitchen, a bar, a stage and a basketball court are included in this modern air-conditioned log structure.

Socially Opened : March 1, 1940 .

- Cabaret Party by the Fort Missoula Officer's Club -

Sponsors - Major & Mrs R.N. Caulkins ; Capt. & Mrs John G. Hill
    Mrs H. Pullium
    Lt. & Mrs George W. Dauncey ; Lt. & Mrs Del Davis

Nine Course Dinner served ; Entertainment by — Buddy McCullough and his team of roller skaters .
    & members of DeRea's School of Dancing

December 7, 1946 : (early Sunday morning) , after an event on the Saturday evening of December 6th - the Log Recreati Center burnt down. (probable cause- bad electrica wiring) :

Fort Missoula Recreation Center Hall

Here is some of the history of this building's existence. The internees were so impressed with this beautiful building that later on it was used for theatrical purposes. To the artists and sailors coming from California, the building itself was a glamorous fantasy dream. This large log building could seat over 800 people, and I would say that for Missoula this was like a "Bijou" theater.

The internees started their own organization. The orchestra, the brass band, the dance troupe, and others began to organize staged "opera" plays that were open to the public. Without bragging too much, considering the times during 1941-1943, for Missoula this was a full-time theater.

I spent most of my time painting and building stage scenery including an altar for Mass.

This hall took away many pains and worries of the sailors who were far away from their families. Besides being a master-level piece of artwork, the hall gave joy and pleasure to the internees, and in many ways, to the community of Missoula itself.

Mr. John C. Moe — A Reflection of the Past

                                    Lolo, MT.
                                    Sept. 11, 1996

Dear Bert:

    Following is my suggested insertions for the first part of your paper.

    Pictured here are U.S. Border Patrol Inspector John C. Moe & wife, Gertrude, a Registered Nurse. John was transferred from the Canadian Border to Fort Missoula on May 6, 1941. Gertrude worked in Whitefish, MT. They were married in St. Anthony's Church, Missoula June 9, 1941. Following their wedding they lived in the second house on officers row at the Fort, until John was called to active duty in the U.S. Navy in October 1941. Following service overseas during World War II, John returned to duty with the U.S. Border Patrol. From 1951-1970 he was a Special Agent in the Federal Bureau of Investigation. He was Sheriff of Missoula County for eight years, 1971-78.

    Pictured here is the wedding of Leonard Kuka and Marian McLaughlin at Fort Missoula on May 16, 1942. Leonard was a member of the University of Montana basketball & football teams, working as a guard at the Fort. Marian was the daughter of Chief Patrol Inspector P.R. McLaughlin. Their wedding cake was made by one of the Italians. Marian also took piano lessons from Italian Joe Paretta.

I HAVE NOT CHANGED THE BALANCE OF YOUR PAPER.

    If I can be of further assistance let me know.

                                    Sincerely,
                                    John C. Moe
                                    7950 Moe Rd. Lolo, MT. 59847
                                         (273-6713)

OUR FIRST HOME

JUNE 1941

HOME

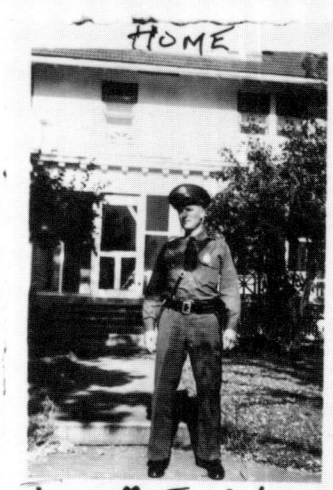

JOHN MOE 6/41

U.S. BORDER PATROL INSP.

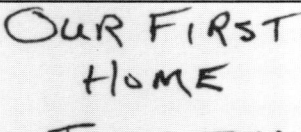

Gertrude H. Axel John C. Moe Are Wed in Missoula

Milltown, June 14.—Miss Gertrude Helen Axel of Whitefish and John C. Moe of Fort Missoula, son of Mrs. Anna Moe of Milltown, were married at St. Anthony's church Monday morning at 7:30 o'clock, with Very Rev. D. P. Meade performing the ceremony.

Mrs. Ted Hill of Missoula, sister of the groom, and M. R. Burns of Fort Missoula attended the couple.

A wedding breakfast was served for the bridal party at the Gehring cafe.

Mr. and Mrs. Moe were tendered a delightful wedding dinner Monday evening at 7 o'clock when Mrs. George Cyr, aunt of the groom, and his mother entertained at the Cyr home.

Seated at a table centered with a huge wedding cake with miniature bride and groom were Mr. and Mrs. Moe, Mr. and Mrs. Hill, Mr. Burns, Mrs. Anna Moe, Mrs. Edith Cyr, Mrs. Andrew Moe, Mrs. Nellie Beavers, Mr. and Mrs. George Lehman, Allan Godbout, Fred Walters, Sr., Mr. and Mrs. Fred Walter, Jr., and children, Eddie and Vera; Mr. and Mrs. George Cyr and sons, George, Donald and Joe.

Mr. and Mrs. Moe received many beautiful wedding gifts. They will make their home at Fort Missoula.

HOME

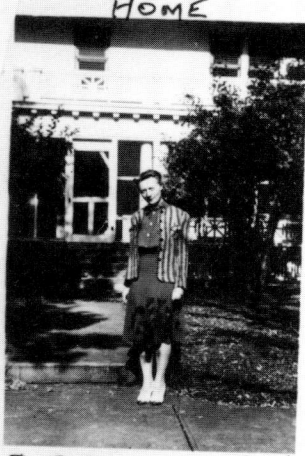

GERTRUDE MOE 6/41

REGISTERED NURSE

Italian Soccer Game

FORT MISSOULA MONTANA ALIEN DET. CAMP

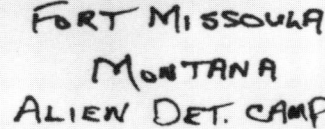

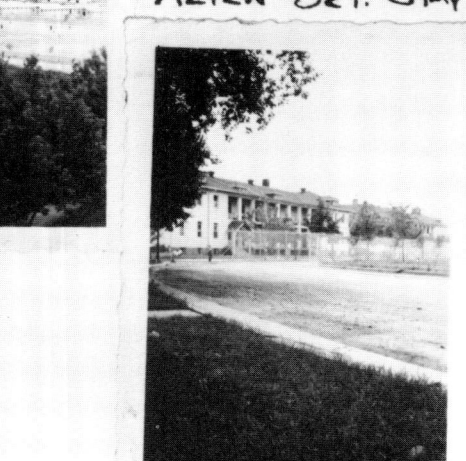

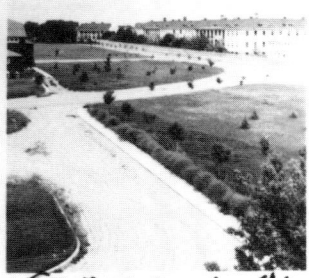

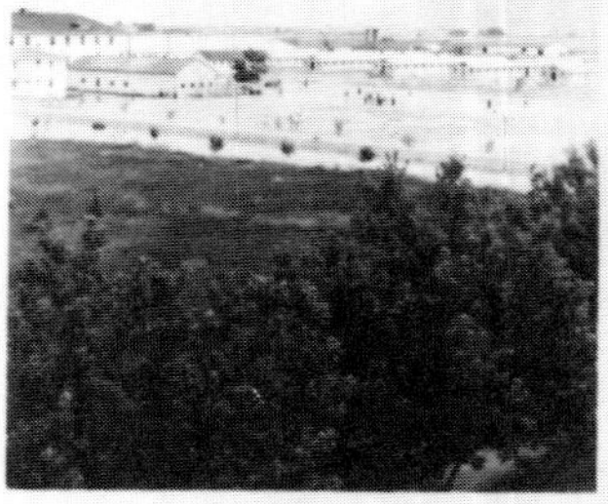

FT MSLA 6-41

JUNE 1941

OUR FIRST HOME
FORT MISSOULA
MONTANA

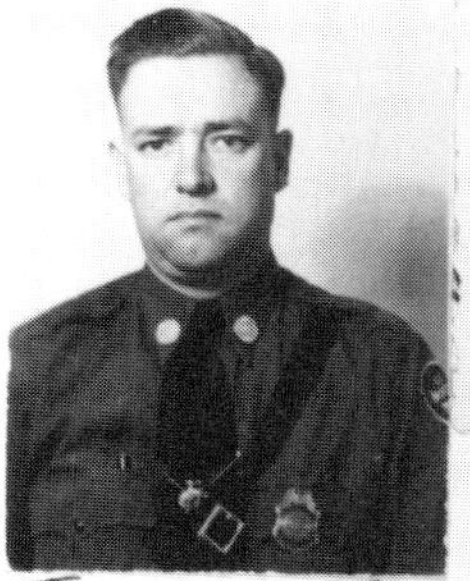

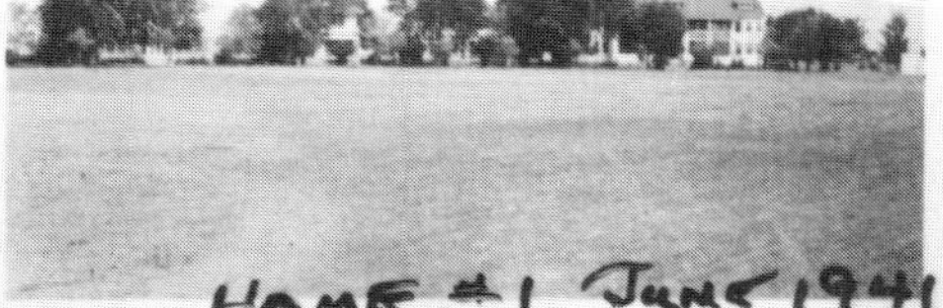

HOME #1 JUNE 1941

JOHN MOE - U.S. BORDER PATROL INSP.

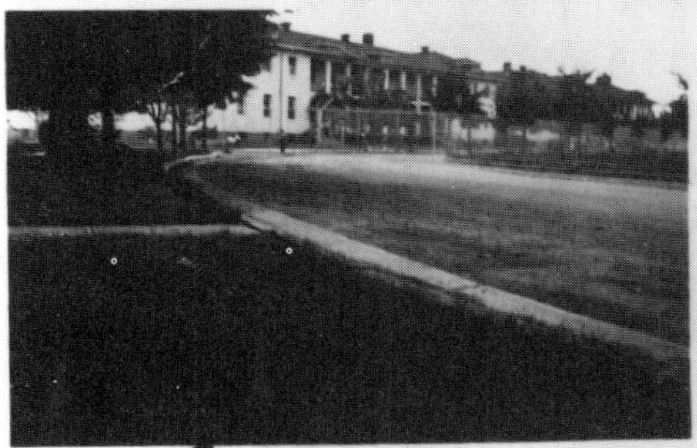

BARRACKS

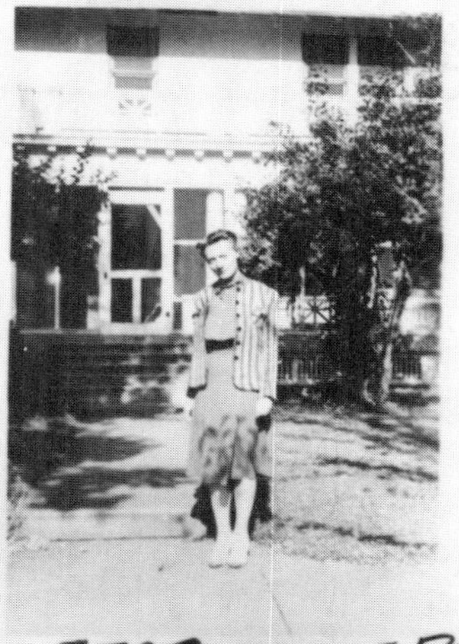

GERTRUDE MOE, R.N.

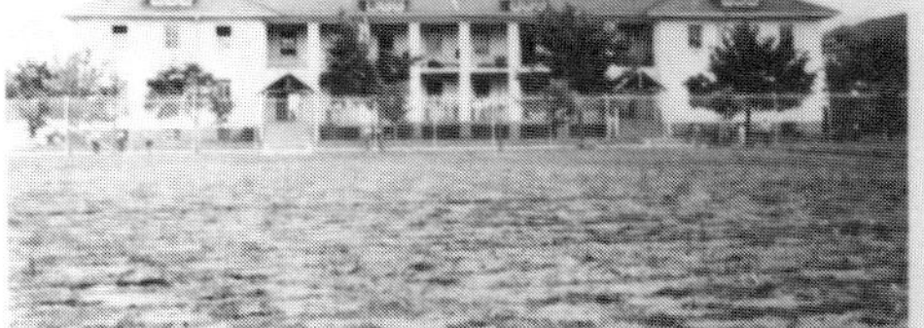

ITALIAN HOME

ALIEN DETENTION
CAMP

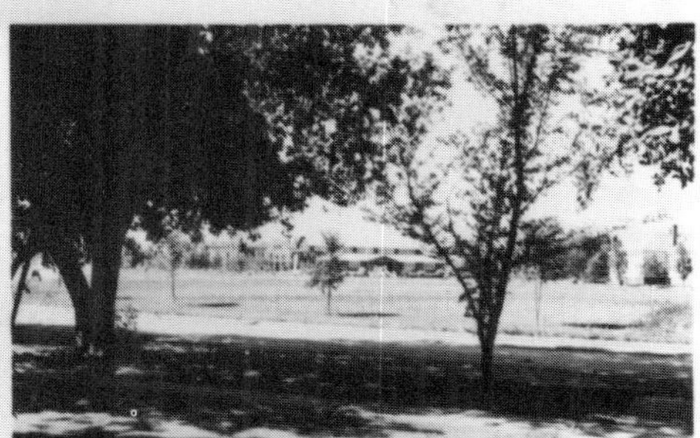

REC. HALL. FT MSLA

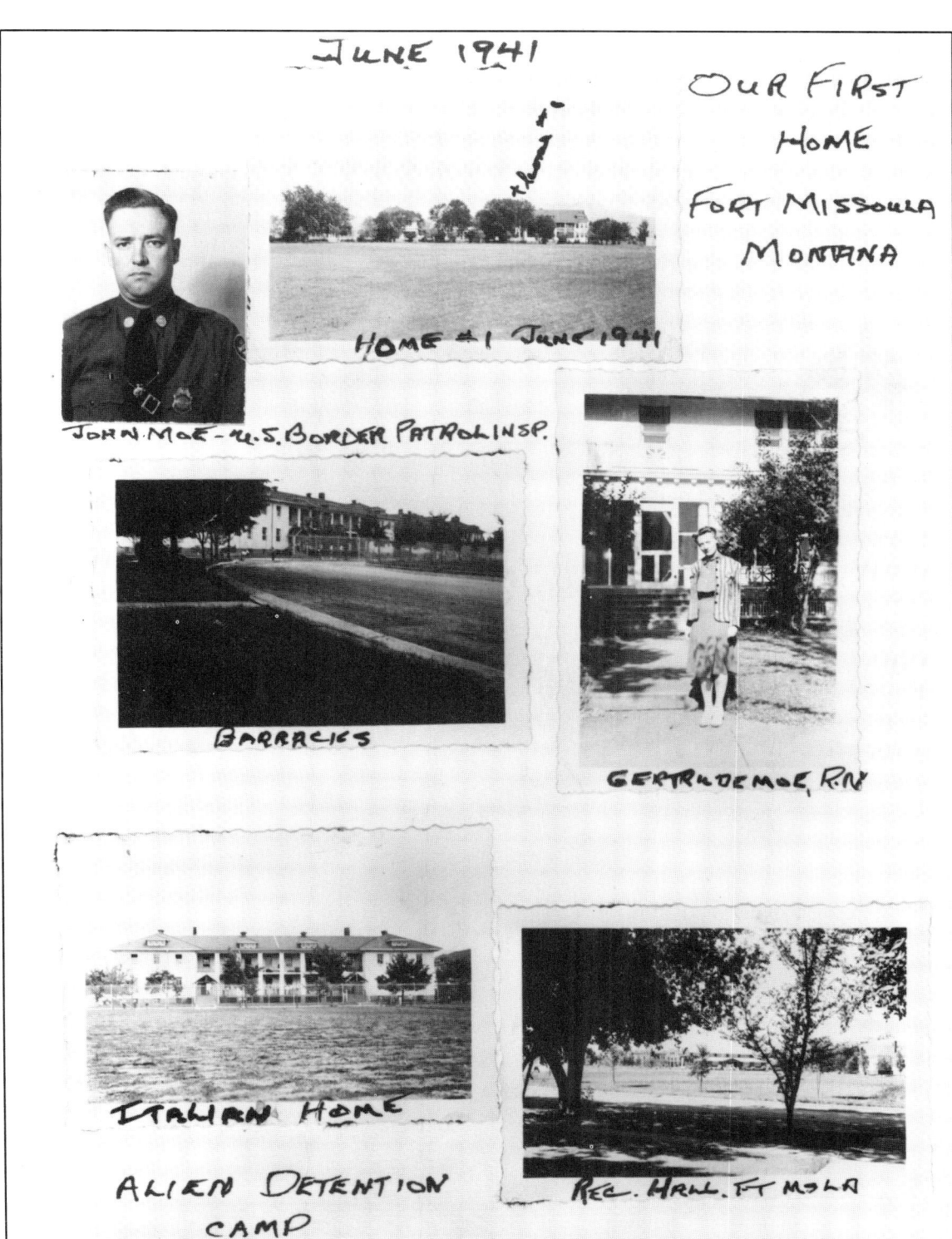

Poem written for a wedding within the Fort—1941-43

> A wedding of all things, is you know.
> So the bribal party made their way
> to the church.
>
> In spite of the inclemency of the weather
> the dear people had assembled.
>
> I had the pleasure of playing the wedding march.
> The bride was lovely, and the bridegroom...
> Please tell me the right word.
>
> Everything passed so beautiful,
> including the weather—and that was the
> Fort of those days.
>
> Umberto Benedetti

Fort Missoula in the 1940s

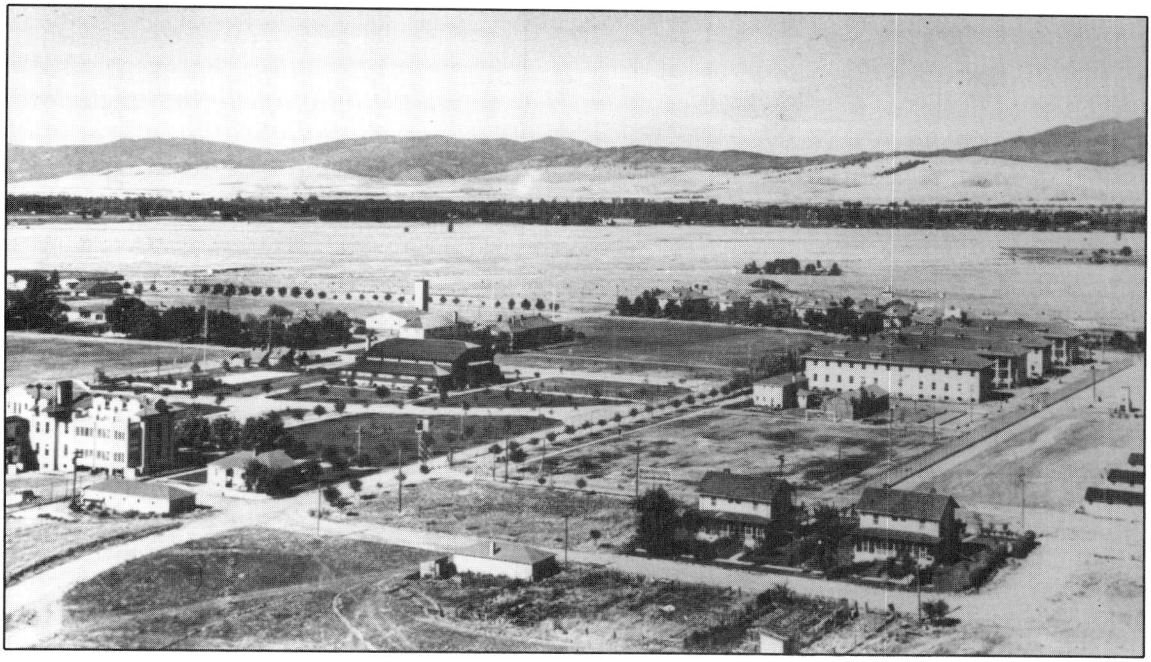

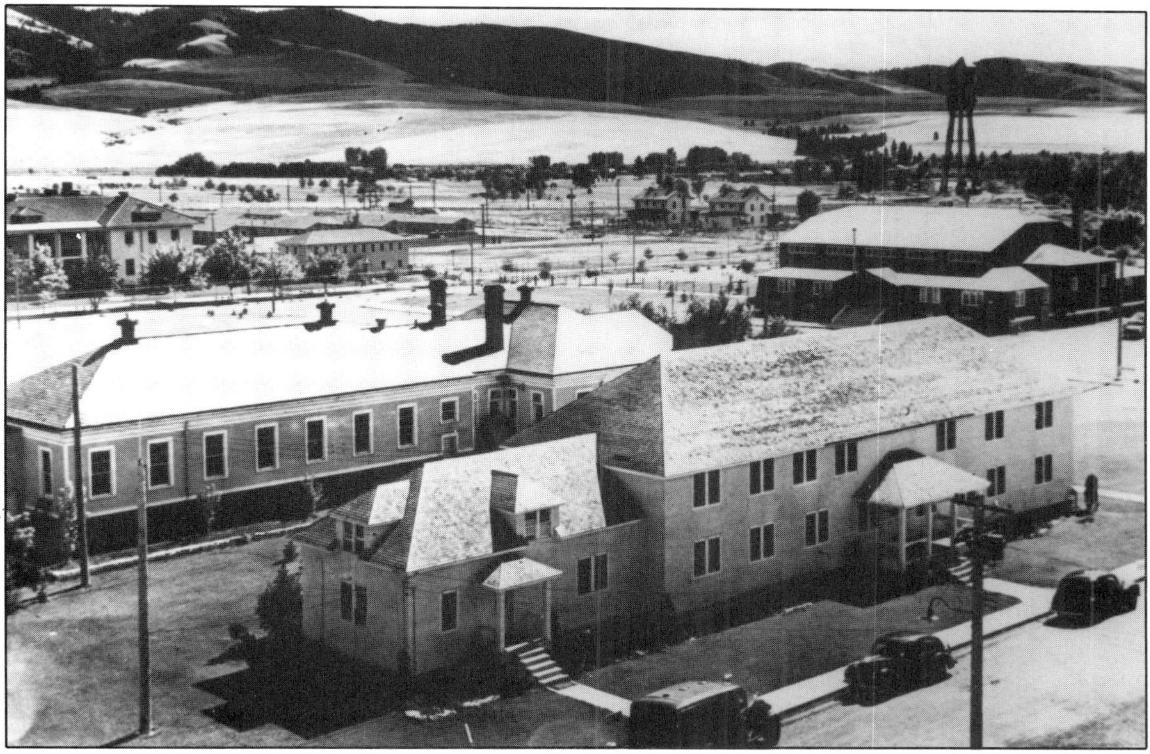

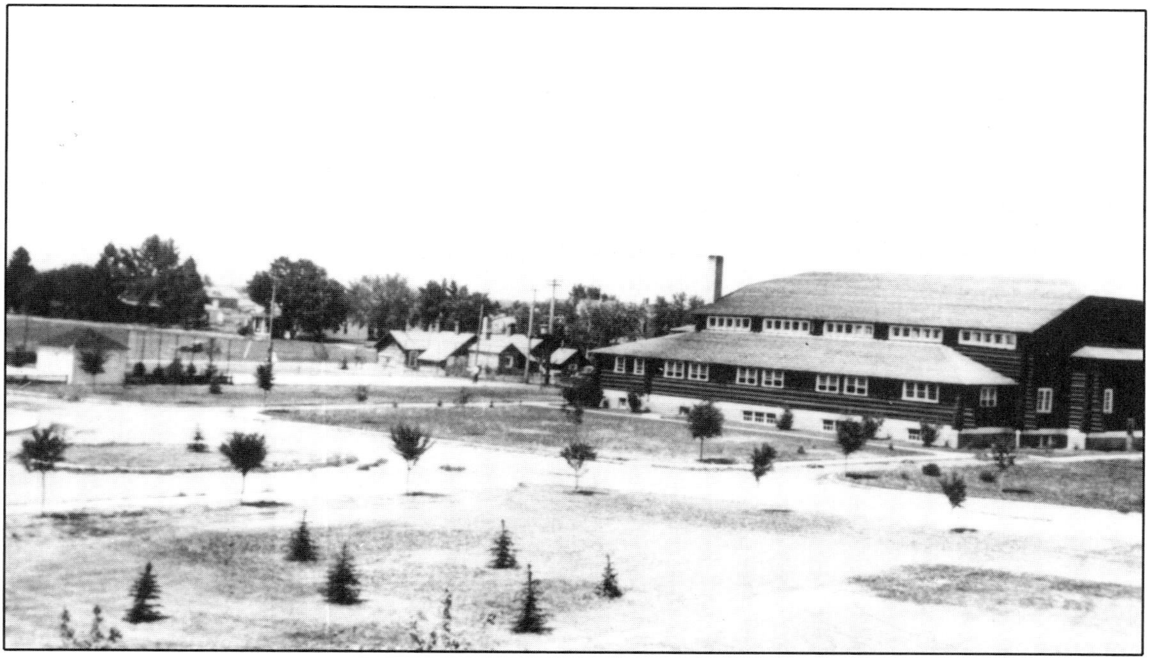

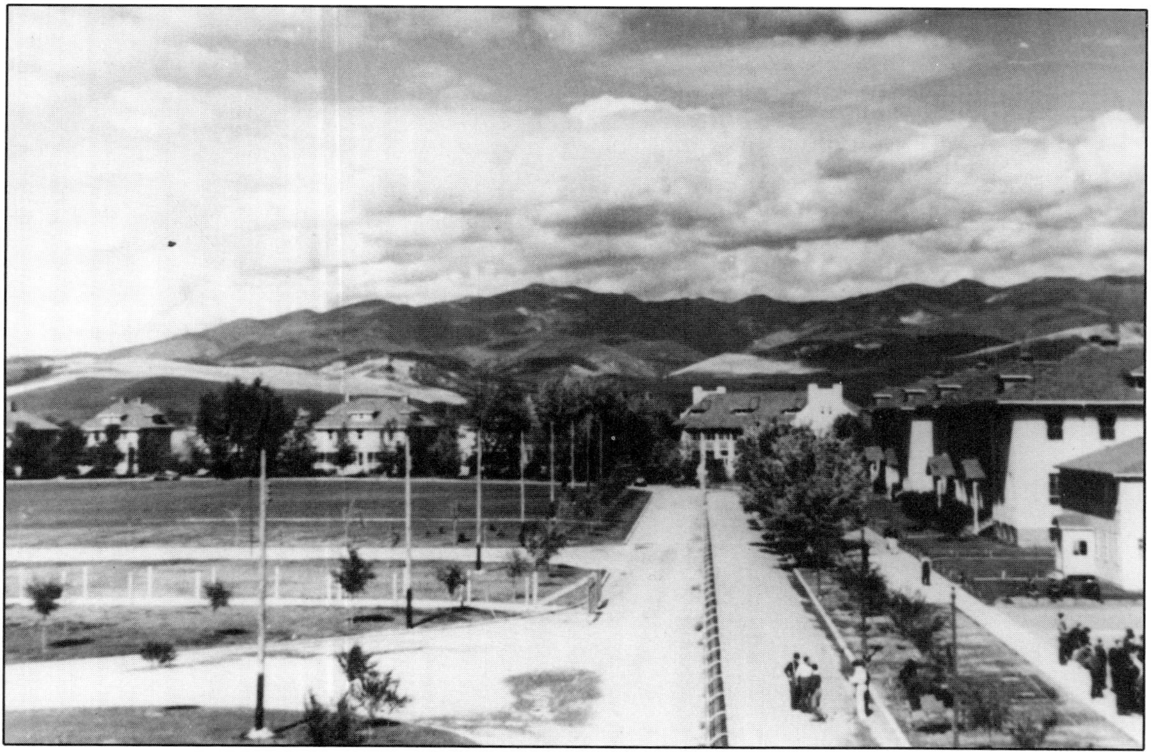

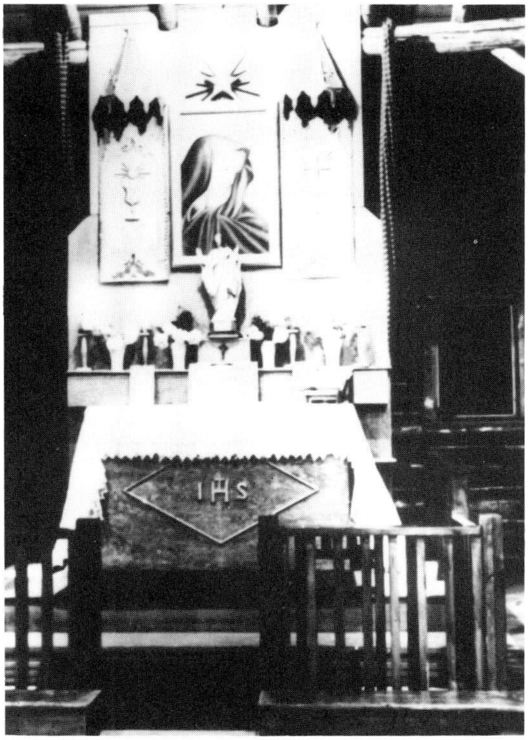
IHS
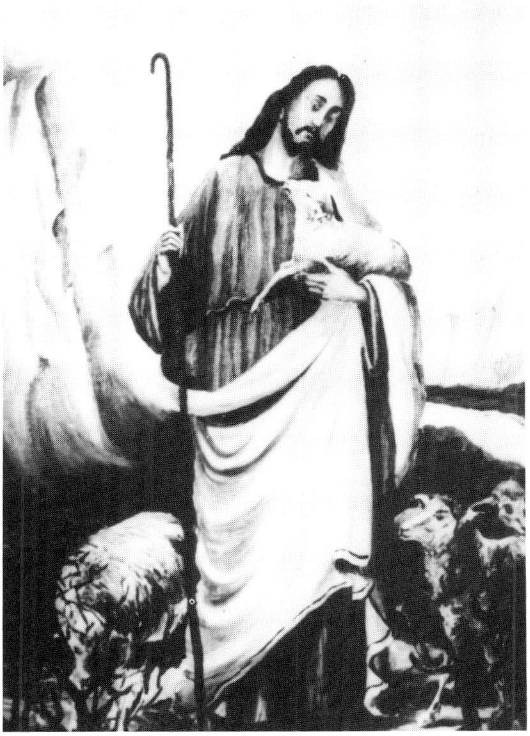
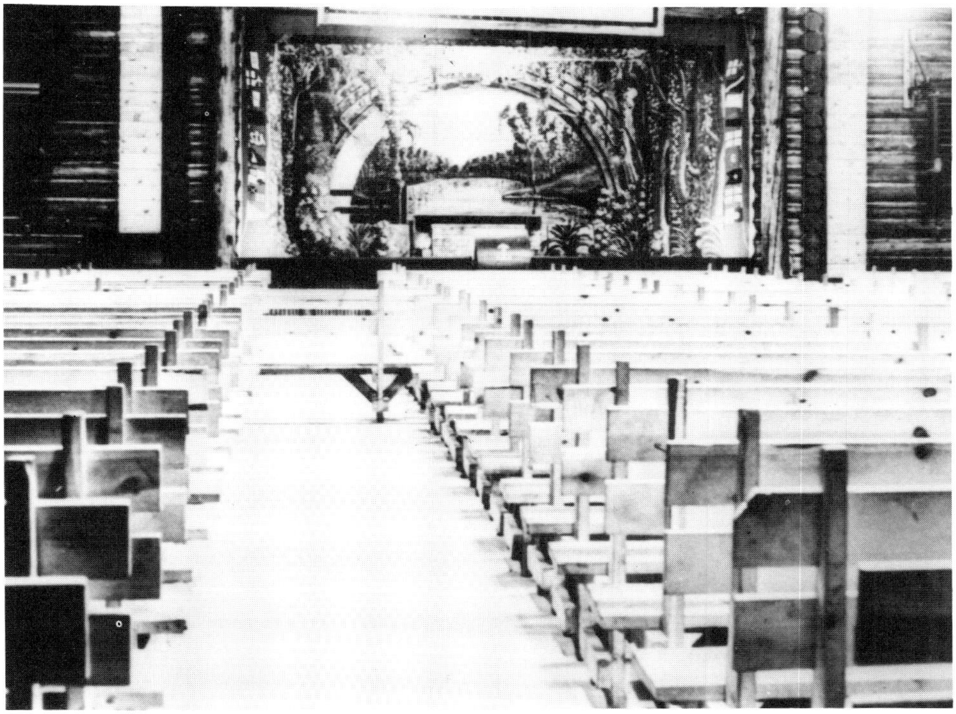

Paintings by the Fort Missoula internees which have now vanished.

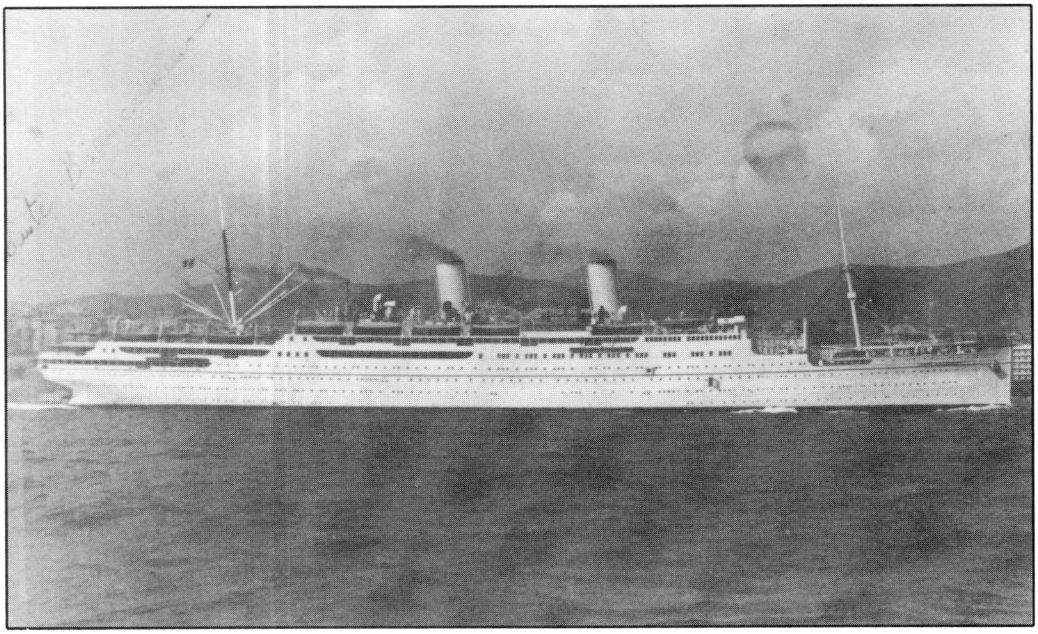

This ship, "Il Conte Biancamano," was a passenger cruiser for the Oriental Line. Among its ports of call were Genova, Gilbraltar, Singapore, Hong Kong, Manila. In 1940, for some strange reason, the ship suddenly abandoned this route for a Central American one.

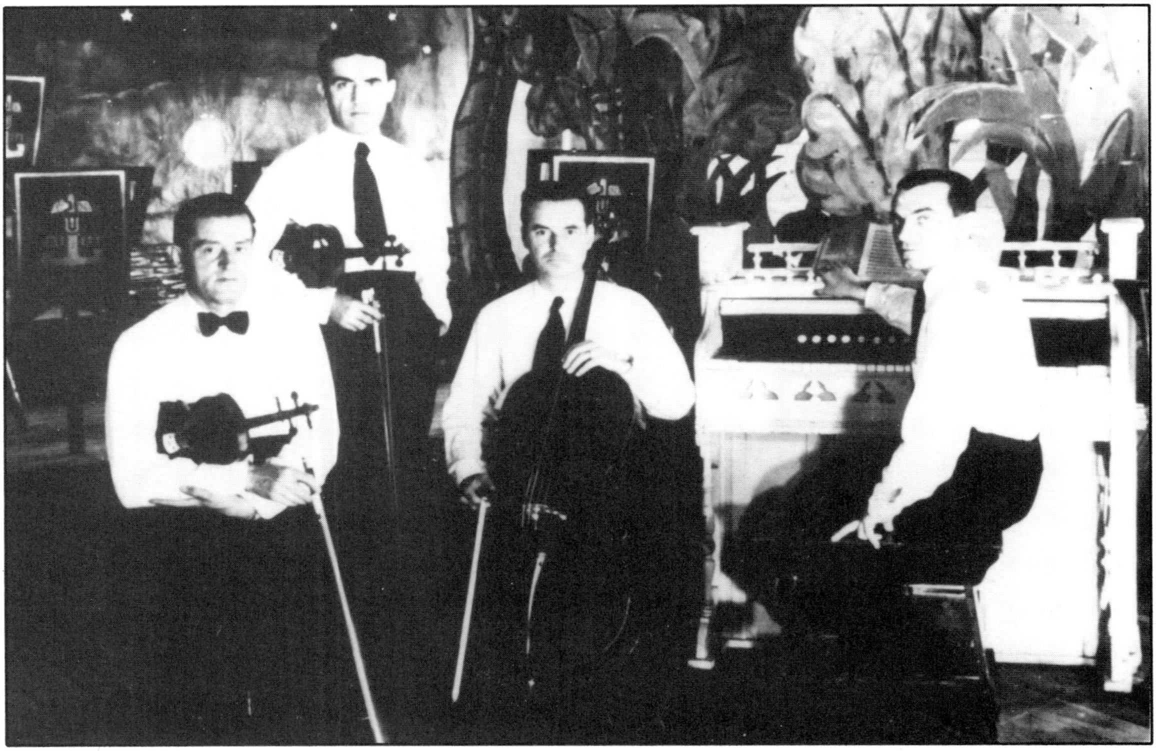

The orchestra of the "IL Conte Biancamano Liner" performed at the Recreation Hall at Fort Missoula for internees and Missoula citizens.

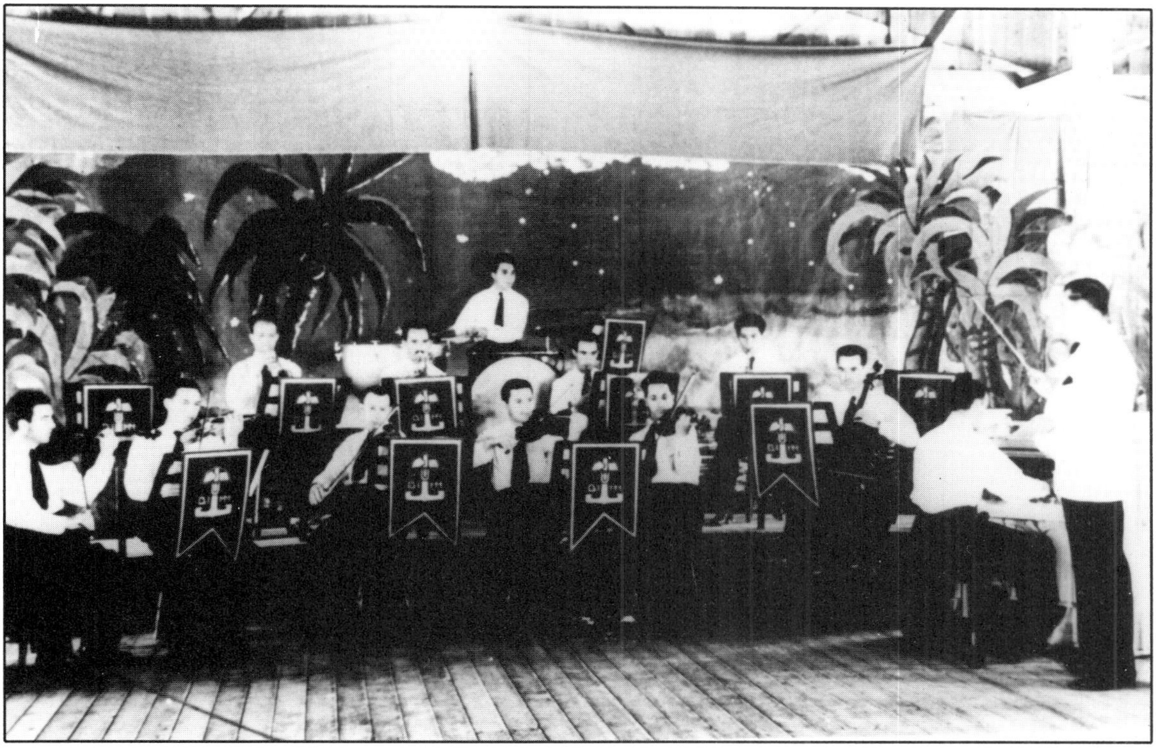

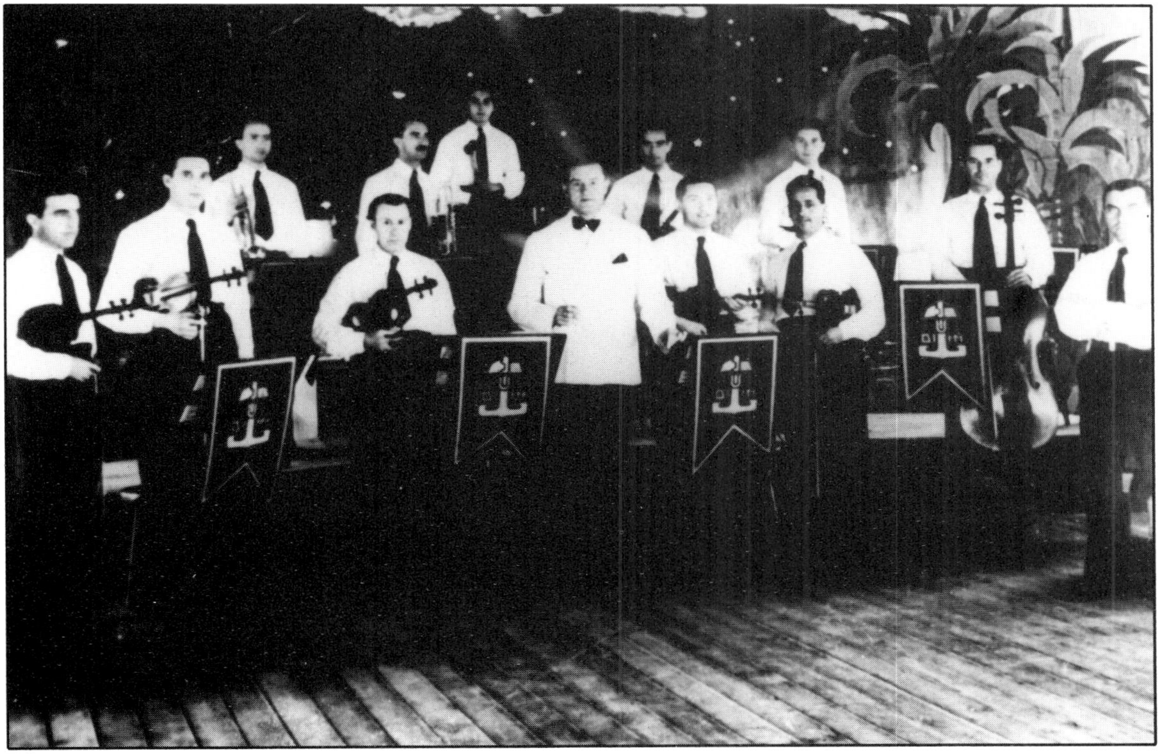

Ship models crafted by internees. Several survive today.

Cleaning the field for a soccer game.

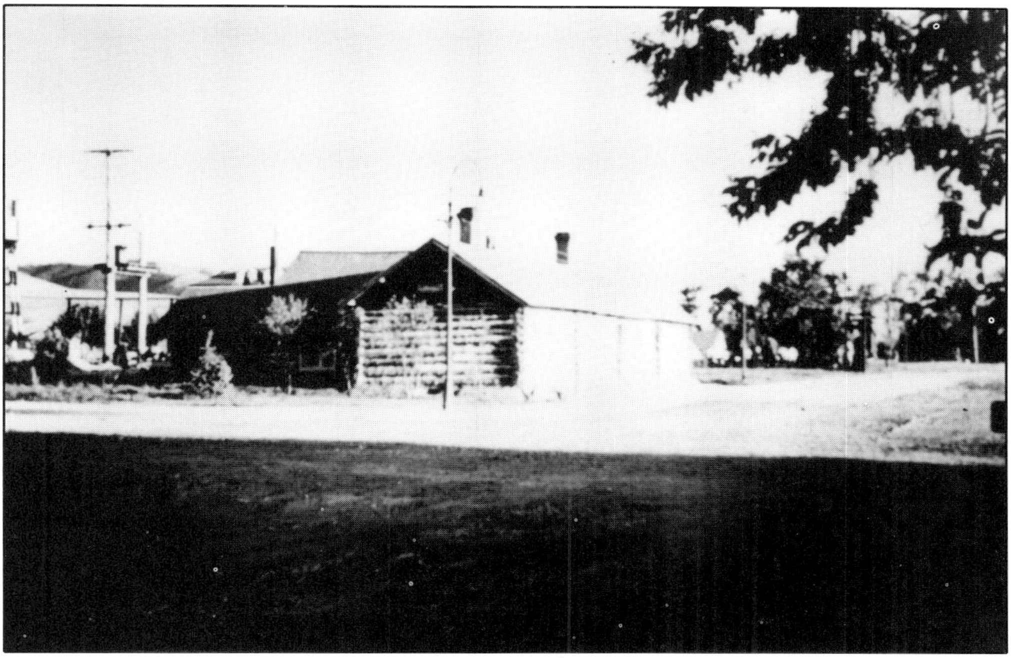

One of the old barracks at the Fort. It may also have been a temporary entrance to the detention station.

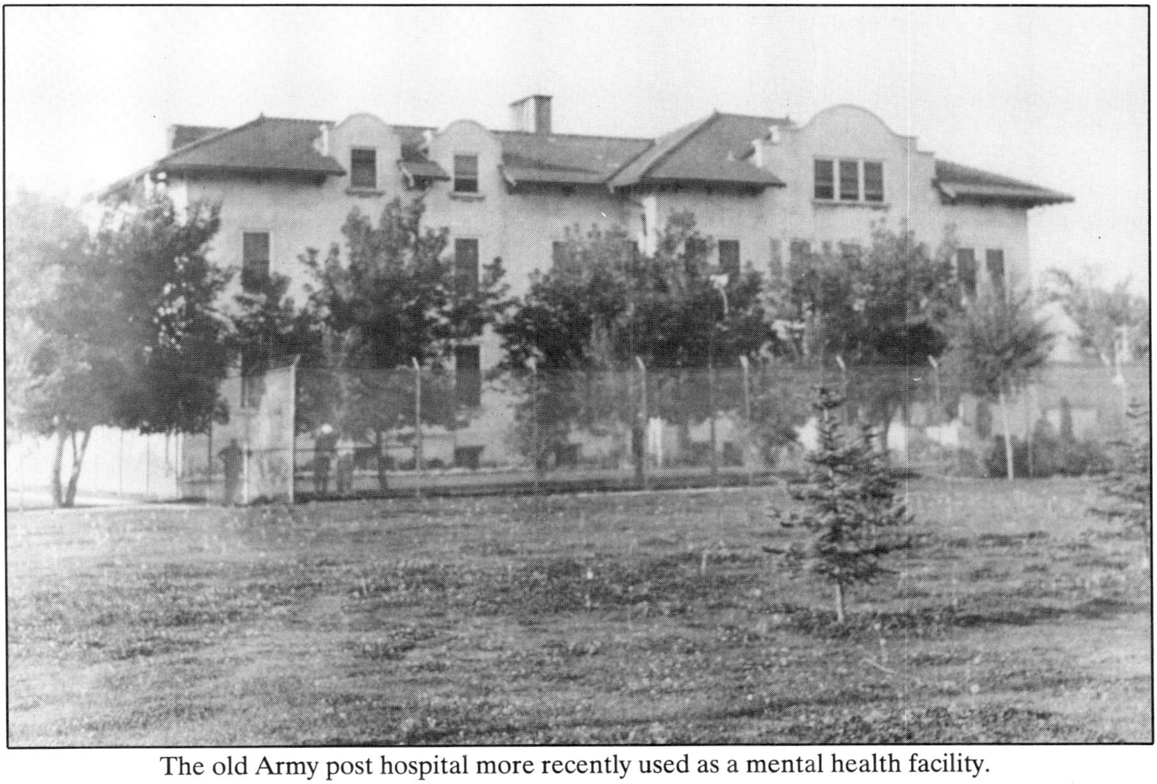

The old Army post hospital more recently used as a mental health facility.

The Joy of Living in Montana

Believe it or not, I have lived in Montana for the past fifty-five years of my life. In my first three years, at Fort Missoula, I fell in love with the surrounding scenery of Montana. Seeing the University of Montana reminded me of the University of Trento in the northern corner of Italy.

I was born in Vasto, Abruzzo, Italy, on the Adriatic Coast. The climate, with the mountains nearby, resembles Montana. Having been in Montana for many years I have found much hospitality and kindness in the people. In Miles City, where I used to teach, at night there is the splendor of the moon as a romantic light to the people of eastern Montana. In Missoula, there is the picturesque beauty of sunset and sunrise. There is a friendly honesty, and they have a fierce loyalty to their land. There are open spaces where you feel the fresh air beating against your face in the mountains.

I met many friendly people in Montana with whom I am still in contact. Montana is unforgettably friendly, and so it was around Black Eagle and Great Falls, where I used to live. Sand Coulee, Trace and Stockett, Malta, Fort Benton, and Glendive, all places I used to go, and Butte, the historical city that gave hospitality to people of all nationalities.

There are beautiful scenarios throughout the forest--streams of creek water, wildflowers of all sorts that make a poetic painting all by themselves, and always the wonderful people in state. From east to west, and north to south, the quality of life is astonishing. If you are curious, Montana can be visited in July, August, and September, when Nature's scenery changes, bringing pure, fresh air. You have passed into the friendly State of Montana!

Even in its present situation, Fort Missoula remains a vision of beauty. Its open space of solitude will cause one to reflect in one's mind on this beauty, and will inspire tourists, artists, and writers.

Springtime in Montana

Do you know Springtime in Montana?
When the roses and flowers begin
To blossom on the street?

When up the gentle hills flow
The tender Bitterroot flowers
With blooming fruit trees?

When Primroses and yellow Daffodils
Gaily cover the Meadows
Bedecked with Gold.

How beautiful are these days
When the Ponderosa Pine sway
In the first warm air with
Meadowlark.

Those hot noon hours
April, May and June.
When the Stone wails
Along the Mountain Trails
Begin to glow gently. And,
The first warm Spring Sun
Is shining in that pleasant
Green Gold of the Bluebunch
Wheat Grass.

How the distant Mountains
Reach toward us, ever more
Blue filled with tender Heart.

****

P.S. All the poems in this book were written in 1941-1943, so I leave the poems as they were written at that time. The readers should grasp only the meaning of the contents, because the writer was not familiar with the English language. "Springtime in Montana" was translated by one of my friends, Dr. Alfonso Manzi-Roma-Italy, a Navy Officer Economist. We were born on the same street in Vasto-Abruzzo-Italy.

Tempo di primavera in Montana

Conoscete la Primavera in Montana?
Quando le strade odorose
s'adornan di profumate rose?

Quando le dolci colline
s'ammantan di verde
e nel soave infinito
lo sguardo si perde?

Quando il tenero Bitterroot accarezza
fiori e tronchi mossi dalla brezza?

Quando le primule e i gialli narcisi
ricoprono,
come tiepida coltre,
i prati
che d'oro sembrano intrisi?

Oh! belleza dei giorni
quando, insieme al Meadowlark,
il pino Ponderosa oscilla
al primo tepore
del sole che brilla!

Oh! dolcezza delle calde ore
del mezzogiorno d'Aprile, Maggio e Giugno!
Quando le pietre dei muri
ai primi calori della Primavera
scintillan lontano
e sui campi impera
il verde-oro del grano!

Dai lontani orizzonti
sembrano giungere a noi
le azzurre cime dei monti
e penetrar con ardore
nella intimità del cuore!

Umberto Benedetti

Fort Missoula Internment Camp

A contingent of internees arrived at Fort Missoula in 1941, carrying some of their belongings. Although the guards were friendly, they were still cautious about everything in that period of wartime. With sailors coming from all parts of the oceans, the guards had strange feelings seeing all the internees; they had never seen such a movement of human beings. For the leaders, guards and townspeople, it was a curiosity.

The camp was well-built, with watchtowers in case of escape attempts. But, on the contrary, most internees welcomed the security of the camp. And, strange as it may seem, after their release some of the internees chose to stay and raise their families in the Missoula community.

This is one part of the Mess Hall at Fort Missoula. These two pictures show how the internees were seated.

The word "prisoners" is an easy word for anyone, including newspaper reporters, because they did not know how to differentiate between a civilian and a war prisoner. The boys at Fort Missoula were not prisoners—they were in a detention camp. They did not serve in any army against Americans. Although they were sailors, they did not know about the war except that they were in the camp, dressed in civilian clothes. But in the confusion and turbulence of that time, reporters could write anything that they had in mind to make the readers happy.

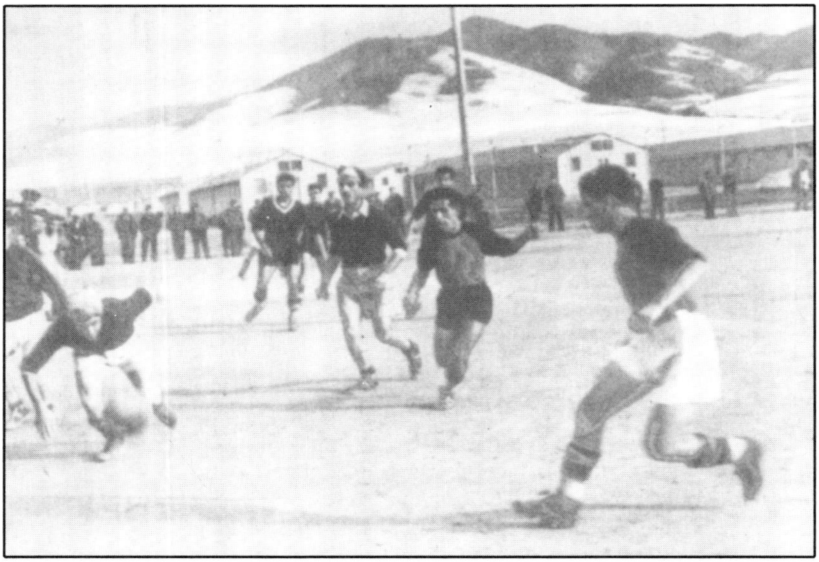

The Italian internees soccer team at the Fort.

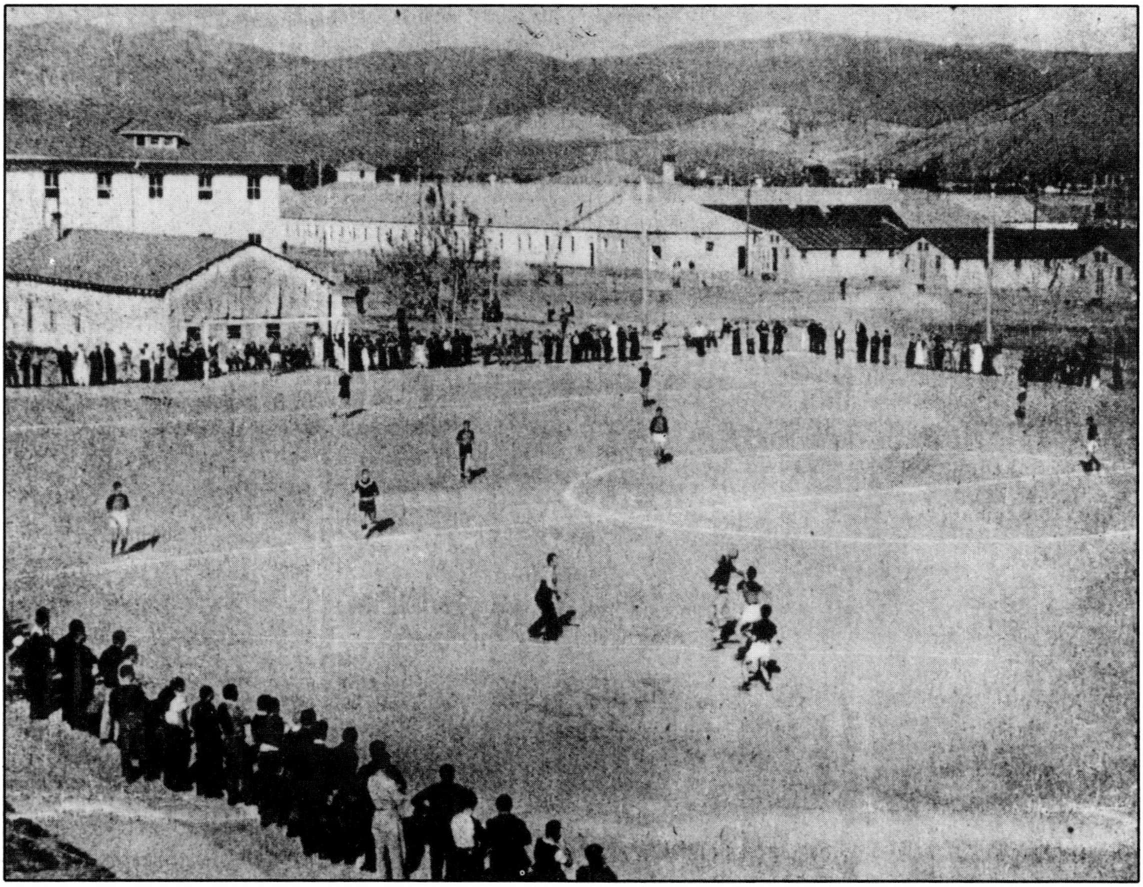

SEZIONE DOMENICALE

CORRIERE D'AMERICA

Part 2 MAGAZINE SECTION

ANNO XX — No. 229 NEW YORK, DOMENICA, 17 AGOSTO 1941 384 Lafayette St., N. Y. City Telefono: ALgonquin 4-1600

LIFE AMONGST THE ITALIANS AT FORT MISSOULA

Bella Vista Has Been Made Into A New City Governed Entirely By Its 993 Seamen And World's Fair Employees

The United States Establishes a New Principle As It Allows Detainees To Create Their Own Municipality in Montana Camp

By GENE REA

(After reading a newspaper report purporting to reveal conditions existng at the detention camps in the United States, Mr. Generoso Pope called his special staff writer and asked him to investigate Ellis Island and Fort Missoula. On the day after the report was published, this writer visited Ellis Island. The next day he took an airplane for Missoula, Montana, and visited Bella Vista. Herewith are the findings which he discovered.)

I went to Ellis Island without making any preparations with the authorities there as soon as Mr. Pope instructed me to investigate the conditions of the Italians being detained in this country by the United States Government. It is important to take into cognizance that under war time conditions no nation in the world can legally deport any aliens to their native country. This is an international law with which the United States is complying. All the aliens being detained in this country are subject to deportation, and, until means are found by which they can be safely sent to their country of origin, the United States must detain them.

When the Ferry reached Ellis Island, none of the immigration officials were expecting a representative from our newspaper. The investigation, therefore, was conducted as a complete surprise and disclosed the average day spent at Ellis Island by the 50 Italians being detained there. Mr. Bryon Uhl, District Director, was pleased to meet your staff writer, and he immediately contacted Mr. Forman to show me around. I was allowed to speak freely with the men. There weren't any guards to overhear our conversation, which was carried on in Italian, nor any official to tell the men what to do.

There is no persecution of Italians at Ellis Island. There is no "bestial treatment" of aliens at this immigration center. There is no spirit of a concentration camp and there are no whips or guns or rough guards to browbeat the detainees into submission. There are no criminals at Ellis Island, nor have any of the officials received any orders to abuse the Italians or any other alien who finds himself detained. The men who have been brought to Ellis Island have not been gathered indiscriminately. They are men who have entered the country illegally and are being detained until their final status is ascertained. The men get good food and sanitary sleeping quarters. Most of the men showed an inclination to become American citizens. The investigation at Ellis Island showed conclusively that the Government of the United States is treating the detainees with human and sympathetic consideration.

Augusto Ricina, who is 29 years old and who came to this country illegally two and one half years ago, seemed to sum up the attitude of all the men when he said: "I want to be an American citizen. I wish there was some way I could become a citizen. If there were an opportunity of my becoming a citizen, I would gladly do anything to get my papers. But they say that there is no law that can make me a citizen".

Your staff writer reported his findings to this newspaper, and a detailed story was published the following day. Then, making reservations for an airplane flight to Missoula, Montana, some 18 hours flying time away, he left for La Guardia airport on the next leg of his investigation.

Missoula, Montana, is situated about 3,200 feet above sea level. Some of the mountains are as high as eight thousand feet. Fort Missoula, which used to be an old army barrack, is situated more than five miles from the airport. It is a little longer from the town, which has a population of 23,000 people. The Fort is situated between the shoulders of mountain ranges. It is protected from the raw wintry colds of other sections of Montana and the northern country because the mountains envelope it and prevent the air currents from becoming too strong. It is a dry and fertile country.

The first sight that I saw of the detention camp was that of a beautiful Summer resort. There didn't seem to be any indication that there was a camp where 993 Italians are being detained. Gradually, as the taxi entered the limits of the Government property a sign indicated that no unauthorized persons would be permitted to enter the camp. When I got there, the official confirmation of my visit from Washington headquarters had not arrived. Mr. N. D. Collaer, Chief Supervisor of all detention camps in the United States (there are three of them) had received my telegram and was waiting for me.

Fort Missoula is indeed a picturesque sight. The homes are solidly built and have Spanish tile roofs. Between rows of trees and the mountain background it presents a colorful [illegible] of a peaceful, thriving community. Fort Missoula consists of some 10,000 government acres. The camp in which the Italians are being detained is, however, fenced in and the detainees live entirely within this "border", which marks the limits of their self-government.

Here again no obtacles were placed in the way of your staff writer in obtaining the needed information. I was allowed complete freedom to do whatever I chose, speak to any one of the men I wanted to speak to, go through their barracks, investigate the sanitary conditions, and take note of their activities. Not once was there a guard to tell me that I couldn't do one thing or another. Not once did anyone tell me that I couldn't speak with anyone of the men being detained.

Fort Missoula is something unusual, for here, in this picturesque surrounding, a new idea has been born. Unlike Ellis Island, the men at Fort Missoula govern themselves. And, unlike the Island, they have a vast stretch of land in which to indulge in any form of activity they choose. So beautiful is the setting that the name of Fort Missoula is no longer being used. Instead this community has become the city of "Bella Vista", with its own autonomous government, protected by the United States.

Bella Vista is outside the control of the Immigration Patrol Guards. They can not enter the confines of the City unless they speak with the "Mayor" or one of the officials. In realty their task is that of a Border Patrol between Fort Missoula and "Bella Vista".

The Italians have, therefore, founded an entirely new community at Bella Vista. They have their own executive and governing bodies. They have their commissioners and deputy commissioners. In the old army barracks at Fort Missoula, a new life can be seen as the 993 Italian seamen and World's Fair Employees are industriously setting about their task of making their government work. Everywhere I saw activity of men preparing for the long winter ahead. New barracks were being constructed, plans were being made for winter sports, social activities, and the problem of heating the quarters.

When Mr. Collaer invited Captains Alessandro De Luca and Francesco La Rosa to visit Fort Missoula last April, he had in mind the creation of a self governing body of officers to take charge of the men who were going to be sent to Montana. The two captains came to Missoula

(Continua a Pagina 2-S)

In commenting on the series of articles now appearing in Il Progresso dealing with the findings of an investigation conducted at Ellis Island and Fort Missoula, Montana, the New York Times, in an editorial published in its issue of Wednesday, August 14th, 1941 wrote:

"A little more than a week ago the Tribuna, published in Italy, printed an interview with Armando Tosi, manager of the Italian Restaurant at the World's Fair, in which Signor Tosi charged that panicky fears entertained here over the fifth column menace had resulted in "bestial treatment" of Italian nationals detained in the United States... Cabled back and published here, as this one was in The Times of August 6, such stories make little if any impression on most Americans. Among the Italian community, however, tales of mistreatment, might, if unanswered cause misgivings.

"Realizing this, Il Progresso, the Italian language newspaper published in this city, sent reporters to interview fifty Italians being held at Ellis Island and to investigate the conditions at Fort Missoula. As was to be expected, the survey showed that Signor Tosi's statement was baseless. Those detained at Ellis Island are persons who entered the United States illegally and who are being held pending determination of their legal status. There are no criminals there.

"At Fort Missoula, where 993 Italian seamen and World's Fair employes who overstayed and cannot be deported under war conditions, are detained, Il Progresso's reporter found neither criminals nor a prison atmosphere, but 10.000 acres of land with "all the characteristics of a Summer resort". Only a handful of immigration officials patrol the camp, he said, and there were no machine guns to be seen. So beautiful is the setting, he reported, that the Italians themselves have named the camp "Bella Vista".

"The articles now appearing in Il Progresso provide an excellent example of the way in which a newspaper can perform a service to its readers by refuting the fanciful tales of propagandists with facts gathered by competent reporters. Il Progresso is to be congratulated on its enterprise."

CORRIERE D'AMERICA — DOMENICA, 17 AGOSTO 1941

(Continuazione dalla pagina 1-S)

by airplane, and when they first saw the site, it so impressed them that they called it, "Bella Vista". That name now stands as the official standard of the new city. When the first group of men came to Missoula in May, 1941, they moved into their quarters and started the work of construction.

Old Fort Missoula, ever since it had been left by the army, had detoriated and needed a complete overhauling. The old barracks had to be thoroughly cleaned. Streets and grading had to be fixed. The grass, which had been allowed to grow wild, had to be weeded and planted anew.

An organization was necessary to carry out the different tasks. Each man had to be put in a position best suited to his talents. An election was held and Captain De Luca was elected "Mayor" of Bella Vista.

The officers elected by the detainees at Fort Missoula are now endeavoring to put into effect the practical end of the Government. It is the task of the Mayor's office to set the machinery in operation. They are entrusted with all executive powers. Any laws or regulations that are to be passed or put into effect must be decided by them.

Although no City Constitution has been formed, and no written laws have been passed, the men at Bella Vista are guided on a purely democratic principle. Any grievances are brought to the attention of the secretaries, who in turn refer them to the proper authorities. These may be any one of the three captains under "Mayor" Captain De Luca, or to the Mayor himself.

The Mayor and his staff, if the problem warrants it, then discuss amongst themselves the best way to solve the problem. If the matter is not urgent, each individual can decide the case and render the verdict. If it involves the City as a whole, then the entire staff resolves the dispute, aided by the Council, which is composed of representatives of the various ships and groups that are now being detained at Bella Vista.

There are twelve departments functioning under the leadership of Mayor De Luca and his executive assistants. They are, the technical department, the postal department, provisions department, materials department, sales department, library deparment, recreational department, orchestra, department of sanitation, the band, religious, and fire department.

All of the work at Bella Vista, excepting the actual construction of the barracks, is done entirely by the 993 Italian "citizens." They cook their own food, serve themselves, adopt any measures to punish guilty persons, organize their recreational and social activities, and provide for their own welfare.

The Government of the United States supplies the men with food, clothing, and lodgings. Each man receives approximately six pounds of carefully balanced food each day. Requisitions are now placed for winter clothing, shoes, underwear, overcoats, gloves, and hats. Outside of this, the citizens of Bella Vista, Missoula, Montana, must depend on their own resources to keep the city going. They must clean it, keep it in good repairs, and maintain law and order, it is only if they do these things that their "freedom" within the borders of Bella Vista are guaranteed them.

Inasmuch as there is not sufficient work for them to keep them occupied all day, the men have ample time to devote to recreation and their own personal handicrafts. The musicians have organized an orchestra which, in the opinion of Mr. N. D. Collaer "is just about the tops." A regular band of 25 pieces also has been organized. A concert was given during the week, on August 16th, in which the community of Missoula actively participated by buying tickets. The money from this was turned over to the Welfare Fund of Bella Vista.

The handicraft of the men at Bella Vista is so artistic that Mr. Collaer went out of his way to speak to the merchants at Missoula to see what could be done about selling these articles to the public. A few of the merchants agreed to cooperate and plans are now being made

~~(Continua a pagina 11-S)~~

N. M.

The next two pages in Italian have not been translated but I summarized them. The 28th of October 1922 was the day the Fascist movement reached Rome. The article states that the internees on that day felt that they were at home in the Missoula camp. They expressed joy to be Italians and some boys said they were Ideologic Fascists. So for one day it was a complete celebration even though the weather was not good. There was a soccer game and many other activities related to that day. The boys kept the flame of faith alive, and faith became a symbol of their power.

IL 28 OTTOBRE A FORT MISSOULA

Ci siamo sentiti in casa nostra.
Ad onor del vero (pur senza intenzione di perdono alcuno),gli amiconi nostri,con una condiscendenza nella quale non speravamo, hanno lasciato fare quello che abbiamo voluto.
Le condizioni del tempo,inutilmente maligne,non hanno influito per nulla sulla completa affettuazione del programma celebrativo che nel suo svolgimento,partecipe la totalita' degli internati,ha dimostrato ancora una volta quanto sia grande il sentimento Patrio ne qui tutti nutrono ed alimentano nei loro petti.
Giornata magnifica,significativa,che ci ha fatto rivivere gli entusiasmi spontanei,sinceri,della prima ora.Che ci ha riavvicinato alla Patria lontana,annullando virtualmente l'enorme distanza he da ESSA ci separa.
Sin dalle prime ore di vita mattutina,il Campo non era quello a tutti i giorni.Lo spirito della solenne data,aleggiante nello ambientefino dal giorno prima,era visibilmente manifesto in tutti. I carateschi "buon principio" s'incrociavano bene auguranti, mentre il braccio si levava in un "saluto romano"piu' virile del consueto. Le vecchie Camicie Nere,gli Squadristi,quelli della Marcia e quelli della"Prima Ora",numerosi fra noi,si cercavano si riconoscevano nelle rievocazioni delle "azioni" del loro tempo,del fulgido tempo,della riscossa.
La pioggerella dispettosa deve essersi rimasta male,quando ha visto il nostro Campo Sportivo occupato dai mille e piu' uomini in solenne raccoglimento attorno all'Altare sul quale il Cappellano Don Bruno offriviva la Messa al Campo.Infatti, stanca della sua fatica inutile,l'ha fatta finita e s'e' di nuovo ritirata fra le nuvole,contentandosi di restare a guardar dall'alto lo spettacolo che sperava guastare nel suo intervento.
Solenni e significative,nella loro fascistica brevita' e chiarezza,le parole commemorative pronunciate dal Comandante del Campo dopo la S.Messa,e quanto mai commovente il defilamento ed il "Saluto Romano" alla Bandiera Nazionale cui faceva scorta d'onore gli Squadristi in Camicia Nera ed una rappresentanza di marinai nelle loro uniforme di bordo,mentre la nostra Banda suonava gli Inni Nazionali e della Rivoluzione.
Intantocla "FONTANA DELLA FEDE" - il simboldwo lavoro che il camerata Prina ha concepito e portato a termine con L'ausilio del camerata Ranalli - aspettavail suo momento solenne e quando,Banda in testa,la colonna si e' portata presso di essa e l'ha circondata applaudendo e inneggiando all'Italia Fascista in Armi eravamo un po' tutti commossi. Non meno commosso era l'Autore ed abbiamo visto tremargli le mani mentre assicurava la Bandierina Tricolore alla "Lanterna".L'accensione del Faro e lo zampillo scaturito dalla bocca del satiro,furono salutati da un lungo applauso e da evviva entusiastiche.Spontanea,perche il Prina,col suo monumentino,ha simboleggiato tutte le cose piu' care al nostro carattere di marinai Italiani e Fascisti.
Non e' forse la vecchia e storica "Lanterna" di Genova quella che a nome di tutta l'Italia porge il primo saluto ai naviganti di ritorno dalle lunghe peregrinazioni su tutti i mari d'oltre oceano? Non sara' forse la "Lanterna" quella che strappera' ai nostri petti un piu' possente # VIVA L'ITALIA",quando i nostri occhi impazienti ne scopriranno la snella sagoma da bordo alla mai troppo veloce nave che ci ricondurra' in Patria ? Non e' forse in nome di quel "Littorio", la cui scure sembra ammonimento e sfida,che i camerati nostri sopportano orgogliosamente il martirio nelle carceri americane ?E quel "Tricolore" piazzato sulla "Lanterna",non e' Esso,forse,il simbolo di tutte le vittorie d'Italia,alla cui ombra sono sorti i Labari e i Gagliardetti dai motti che sono giuramento ?
A ben ragione il camerata Prina,- la tua mano tremava ed i tuoi occhi luccicavano nel pianto stretto fra i denti e non eri solo a sentirti il cuore in bocca,perche' tutti,come te,avevano gli occhi sulla Bandierina ed il pensiero alla cara Patria nostra, alla casa amata,alla famiglia,alle Eroiche Legioni che gloriosamente combattono per l'Italia in obbidienza alle supremi leggi di ROMA !
E del resto,non ha detto e dice tutto da se' il continuo alternarsi di pose fotografiche di cui la "FONTANA DELLA FEDE" e' diventata l'ambito sfondo ?

Il programma delle manifestazioni non poteva e non doveva mancare della parte sportiva e ricreativa. Il pomeriggio, infatti, i nostri AZZURRI e ROSSO-NERI ci hanno fatto assistere ad una animatissima quanto composta partita di calcio, conclusasi con un cameratesco...uno a uno.

La "LOTTERIA" che ha seguito immediatamente la partita di calcio e che si e' protratta fino alle diciotto, e' stata anch'essa motivo di una riunione generale animatissima (....Ragazzi, non spingere). Tutti hanno voluto "pescare" il loro biglietto-premio e tutti hanno seranamente fatto buon viso a cattiva sorte. Purtroppo i premi allettanti non potevano essere di piu' di quanti erano e quindi pochi fortunati, ma nessuno se ne e' andato a mani vuote. Qualcuno avrebbe preferito (diciamo cosi) che i vestiti, oppure i panciotti, o i cappelli, o le camicie, fossero stati..... mille e quaranta, ma cari miei dal pezzo di sapone o dal pacco di fiammiferi, purtroppo questo non era materialmente possibile; o poi ......me lo chiamate poco il detto "sfortunato al giuoco, fortunato in amore"?

Siamo poi certi che la viva bellezza della manifestazione serale, vi ha fatto dimenticare li ingiustizie della sorte.

L'apprezzabilissimo lavoro dei volenterosi incaricati dello addobbo del Teatro, ci ha fatto domandare a noi stessi se eravamo proprio... qui.

Scritte e motti fascisti, frasi salienti degli storici discorsi del DUCE, Bandiere Nazionali e le effigi di S.M. il RE e del DUCE biancheggianti in grande Fascio Littorio in campo nero sormontante il boccascena, sono stati il motivo piu' bello della nostra soddisfazione, ed il colpo d'occhio all'entrata nella Sala, si ripercuoteva sul cuore, nell'animo, per risalire sul volto di tutti in un'espressione di gioia-intima, spontanea e serena, ma non priva di fierezza.

Piu' adatta di cosi non poteva essere la scelta del camerata Mo. Dall'Aglio nel programmare la prima parte della serata, con la quale ha presentato i ben affiatati cori che molto hanno meritato le scroscianti applausi al termine di ciascun pezzo.

Il famoso coro del Nabucco, col quale il Verdi interpreto' lo spirito del Rinascimento Nazionale a dispetto dell'Arciduca Francesco, ha assorbito tutta l'anima nostra, facendola palpitare di patri e sacri sentimenti. Cosi il coro de "I Lombardi" dello stesso italianissimo Verdi e non meno commovente la "Preghiera" del Mose' di Rossini, ispirata dai vivissimi sentimenti patri che l'irredentismo dell'epoca sapeva far trapelare in ogni modo e con ogni mezzo, malgrado l'accorta e severa vigilanza dei "cecchini". L'"INNO A ROMA" dell'immortale PUCCINI, eseguito con vero trasporto, ha portato al culmine l'entusiasmo dei presenti. Entusiasmo e commozione, manifesti attraverso un applauso prolungato e nutrito, soltanto interrotto quando i cori hanno accennato ad iniziare un altro canto. Un canto d'attualita' tutta nostra: "L'INNO DEGLI ITALIANI INTERNATI A FORT MISSOULA". Le parole con le quali il camerata Guidi, intelligentemente e con sentimento, ha messo insieme quest'inno, sono l'interpretazione precisa dell'animo di noi tutti che, silenziosamente, decorosamente orgogliosi ed animati da fede immensa nella Patria Vittoriosa, subiamo e sopportiamo un'ingiusta prigionia.

Bella la musica che il Mo Dall'Aglio ha appropriato alle parole del Guidi e perfetta l'esecuzione corale che meglio non poteva meritava il plauso unanime ed entusiastico dei presenti.

Un bravo di cuore ai nostri cantori ed al loro egregio maestro

La seconda parte della serata ha compreso diversi numeri di canto ben sostenuti dai camerati Cipolato e Massabo', ai quali si sono alternati i camerati Fossano e Bergamini con alcune argute e divertenti macchiette. L'ottima preparazione di questo genere teatrale e' opera, come sempre lodevole, del camerata C.Graziani.

Ha concluso la seconda parte del programma, un Canto in versi sciolti, scritto dal Bergamini e monologato dal Guidi, intitolato "VENTENNALE". Ogni commento a questo lavoro con cui l'Autore ed il suo valente interprete hanno saputo infondere nell'uditorio nostalgia, commozione ed entusiasmo, sarebbe superfluo. Diciamo soltanto che e' stato coronato da un vivissimo e prolungato applauso e che tanto il Bergamini che il Guidi continuano a raccogliere parole meritatissime di plauso e di compiacimento. Alle quali vogliamo aggiungere ancora le complimentazioni de "LA FIACCOLA" che, ben volentieri, dedica il meritato spazio fra le sue pagine al "VENTENNALE", non solo per la bellezza delle parole che ci e' grato restino nella nostra raccolta, ma anche ad uso dei moltissimi che ne hanno chiesto copia.

Adjustment Within the Camp

The first year in the camp at Fort Missoula was not very good because, although the government sent all kinds of supplies, it still was 1941 and the war was full-scale. The officers were bewildered and confused. When Captain Robert Frazer came to take charge of the campus, we then had all necessary supplies and everyone was happy. Of course, with 1,200 sailors and Japanese civilians it was very difficult to make everyone happy.

The Judicial Commissioners classified each of the internees by alphabetical order, depending on their answer in the hearing. Those classified "A" got the best places when they went to work, without being watched. Those classified "B" were more or less with the bosses, and those classified "C" were supervised on the railroads, forests and farms by their bosses. However, there came a period of time when no one had to be supervised because their attitude and behavior were like friendly workers. It should be understood that in that period of time America desperately needed laborers. Therefore, the mentality of the supervisors began to change and they got good results based on the work they did. Also, after 1943, a few of the internees served in the United States Army, and some signed on for twenty years and got married while they were in the Army.

A LITTLE SAIL BOAT

A LITTLE WHITE PILGRIM SAIL
IS SET OUT TO FIND A SMALL BEACH.
IN HER FULL HEART SHE IS NOT DISCOURAGED
FROM SAILING THE SEAS.

A LITTLE SAIL, HUMBLE AND MODEST
UNDER THE ARCH OF CONSTELLATIONS,
A NEST OF SORRY SONGS
UNDER A STORMY WIND WITH NO PROTECTION.

A LITTLE SAIL WITH A MONASTIC JOY
KNEELING IN THE RAINBOW HORIZON
THIRSTY BY A CLEAR WATER FOUNTAIN
OF LIGHT THAT FALLS DOWN FROM A STAR.

A LITTLE SAIL, FULL OF DESIRE,
THE DEAD BITE YOUR WOOD;
BUT WHEREVER YOU GO, MAKE YOUR MARK
WHITE IS THE NAME OF GOD AND COUNTRY.

*****

These four stanzas of poetry were written while I was in the Fort Missoula Camp.

These Boats "Ran Through the Rivers"

I do not intend to offend anyone, but as you can see by the photo below the 1990s idea of "A River Runs Through It," was not a new one. The internees (not prisoners) built two boats in 1941 to use on the Bitterroot and Clark Fork rivers that flow near the fort. No one knows what became of these boats. The boys who built the boats did not know the English language, but I'm sure they would be surprised, after fifty-five years, to see all the newspapers and advertisements printed concerning the rivers. They named the boats "Venezia" and "Trieste" after towns from their Italian homeland.

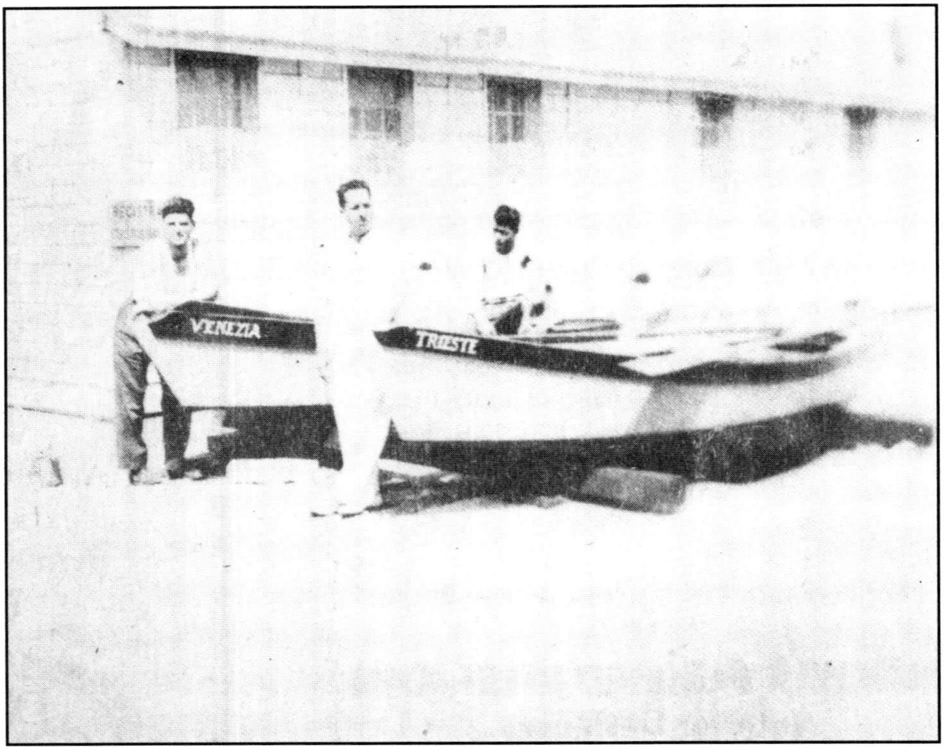
VENEZIA
TRIESTE

A Comment to the Comments

This comment was written by Alessandro De Luca, the first Mayor of the Fort Missoula Internment Camp, 1941-1943, and was translated by the author in Missoula, Montana in 1995.

There were groups of theatrical artists in the Fort. They put on a stage play called "La Fiaccola." The internees took a lot of criticism, as usually the Italians do about any work that comes out for the first time. I don't remember if the work was on stage or if it was in the camp's newsletter. Besides the sailor internees, there were 250 to 260 civilian internees coming from all over California. At any rate, in response to the criticism, the Mayor of the camp responded in his own way. Here is what he said:

An Excerpt, or Philosophic Thought

Only the creations of Nature are perfect, because only Nature knows what should be done. The creation of man, even if it is perfect in concept and in intention, in reality always has some faults to be corrected and abolished in the course of life through the same creation itself.

Nothing is strange, and so even in "La Fiaccola," that today is presented for the second time, there is some imperfection by our community. I say "all" because it is not the case to be criticized by a few professionalists who are not satisfied just because (in general) there are some defects. These critics have their own defects. Why don't these people who criticize the work write something every week in regard to the "Opera?"

The Editor's Office sooner or later should leave some space in the four pages of the camp's newsletter for the criticism or comments.

We must understand that the camp's newsletter should not be a news compilation. The newsletter was created for the camp and was baptized "La Fiaccola" because the name means the silent faith that we have our souls. It was born for the camp, and should reflect life in the camp through articles and pictures and other annotation.

Leave the argument of politics and editorial comments to the professionals of the free press. The events of war are reported every day by the radio news, as well as other commentators. Therefore, let the voice of Rome have the right to say what it wants, and it is up to us to listen and believe.

That is enough for us, don't you think so? Then, when we go back to work we should give what we can to "La Fiaccola, but it must be only material that comes from the camp. The editors can make exceptions to this, but the material should be their own work.

I conclude with a few words for the amateur poets and writers. We have within the camp a good library that will provide abundant research into the best Italian poets. Do you understand me? Therefore, let us go to work in a spirit of friendship and cooperation.

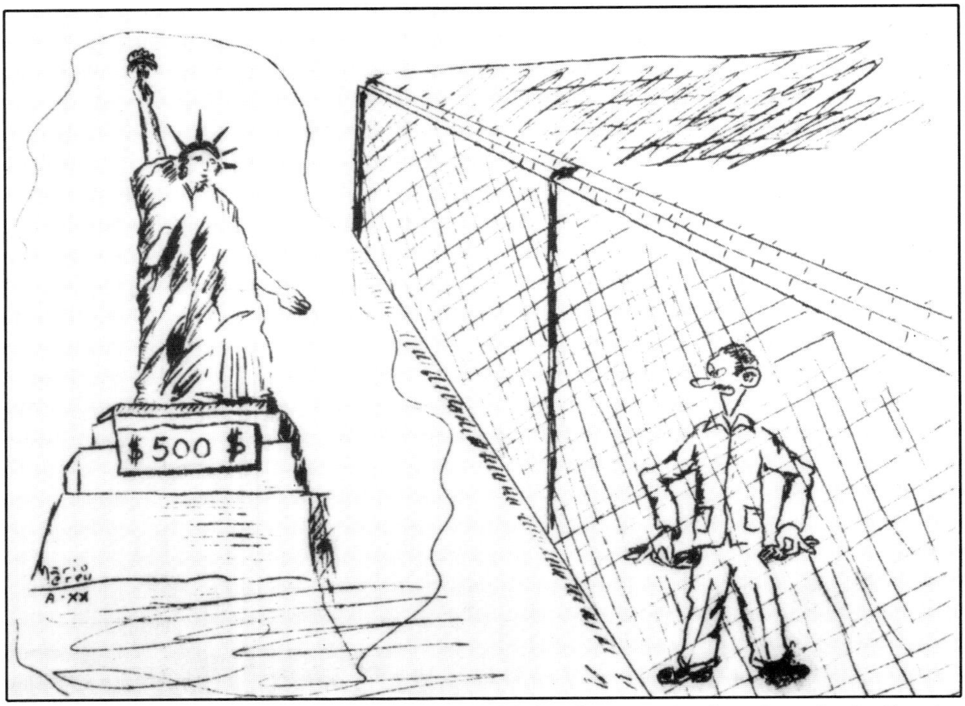
$500 $

This pictures expresses some humerous words and jokes because in that time the Italian internees arranged a theatrical play named "La Fiaccola," which is satirical and humorous per se.

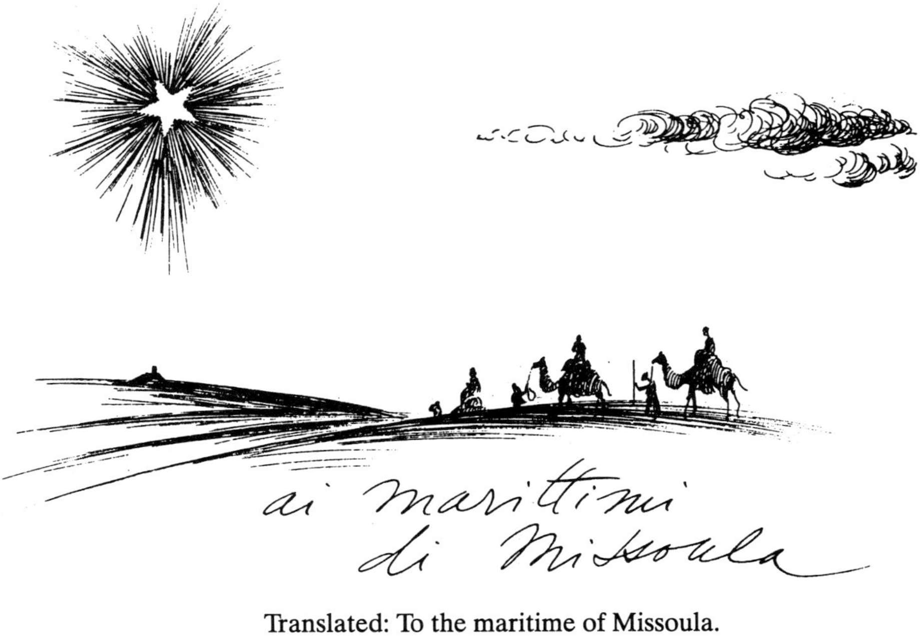
ai marittimi
di Missoula

Translated: To the maritime of Missoula.
A Christmas greeting to the maritime of Missoula.

"COMANDANTE G.LOCATELLI.STAZIONE DI DETENZIONE.POST 1539.FORT MISSOULA MONTANA."

"VOSTRO TELEGRAMMA MAGGIO 30.NOSTRA LETTERA MAGGIO 19 DICHIARAVA IMPOSSIBILITA' RIMPATRIO INTERI EQUIPAGGI.LEGAZIONE COMUNQUE,SECONDO LETTERA MAGGIO 22 CONSIDERAVA POSSIBILITA' RIMPATRIO PRIMARIAMENTE DEI VECCHI,DEI MARITTIMI AMMALATI,E DEGLI IMPIEGATI Ex-FIERA MONDIALE.CUI NOMI VENNERO SOTTOPOSTI AL DIPARTIMENTO DI STATO.A CAUSA DI LIMITATISSIMO SPAZIO A BORDO NESSUNO DEI DETTI RICHIEDENTI E' STATO INCLUSO NOSTRO MALGRADO.NEL SECONDO VIAGGIO SCAMBIO DEI PRIMI DI GIUGNO.MA CONTINUIAMO I NOSTRI SFORZI PER UN TERZO TRASPORTO.ONDE FACILITARE IL NOSTRO LAVORO FAVORIRETE INVIARE PRIMO.NUOVA LISTA COMPLETA DI TUTTI I CITTADINI ITALIANI AL CAMPO INDICANDO ETA',OCCUPAZIONE,INDIRIZZO DI CASA.SECONDA LISTA DEGLI UOMINI OLTRE I SESSANT'ANNI OLTRE AD UNA DEI MARITTIMI AMMALATI DESIDEROSI DI RIMPATRIO,TERZA LISTA DEGLI IMPIEGATI EX FIERA MONDIALE RIMPATRIANTI.QUARTA LISTA DI ALTRI DESIDERANTI RIMPATRIO.TUTTI COLORO CHE HANNO GIA' RICHIESTO IL RIMPATRIO DOVREBBERO ESSERE AGGIUNTI ALLA LISTA.FAVORITE SPIEGARE SITUAZIONE ALL'INTERO GRUPPO ITALIANO AL CAMPO E D'INFORMARLO CHE LA LEGAZIONE CON LA PRESENTE ACCUSA RICEVUTA DELLE NUMEROSE RICHIESTE INDIVIDUALI RICEVUTE PER TELEGRAMMA E LETTERE AEREE E RICONSIDERERA' AL PIU' PRESTO LE LORO RICHIESTE DI RIMPATRIO COL DIPARTIMENTO DI STATO.   LEGAZIONE SVIZZERA."

This letter is from one of the captains of the boat *G. Locatelli*. With this letter he communicated to the authorities and the Swiss delegation the condition of sailors, their health and their age. The captain asked the authorities if something could be done or some arrangements made for the sick persons.

Theme

This is a dream of literary prose telling the story of Viola, written on February 4, 1942 at Fort Missoula, Montana, when I was an internee. Viola means "Primavera—Spring Flowers," with a variety of colors, and also refers to one you loved in the past. This can be judged as a lyrical, or informal, essay because it is a personal dream.

Viola, what sad charm holds your soul, that once I was loved by you. In the shadow of my room a strange, dully person is inside me. I don't like to remember even with a slight idea, but after wandering around, the memory came back immediately. It was the motive of my oppression that the name of a woman, a modest scent of flowers, came to my mind. Viola, so near and yet so far. Thus began my slow fantasy to remember the thing that came so close to me and then went away by itself.

The springs flowers, la primavera, adorned the earth like a beautiful ornament; it was a festival of natural flowers, of green and song. Even you enjoyed that beautiful ornament, and your soul was laughing, springing into youthful life with hope and rosy dreams; after a sighed love on my silence and unknown love. I throw my arrow full of fire, my arrow heated you, and began our love. Oh, how long . . . . Can it not be forgotten?

How many remembrances I had of those youthful days in the country, along the beach, and around the mountains. Everything is finished; it was your whim that you thought you were beautiful and admired by everyone. It was because of the frivolous pleasure of new emotion that I lost you. I could not suffer any more to see you go with other lovers. My jealous envy of your beauty was consuming my existence. So I lost because of my stupidity. Here I am in my room alone with my pain. I cannot persuade even myself that your lips in the days long ago used to belong to me. I could not see you with lovers. Even you, you don't feel. Don't you remember that moment, the kisses that you gave to that intruder, on the one day you were only mine?

Viola, you still have something of me on your body, in your soul. Think about me with that sweetness that remains in your spirit. Pause for a moment sometimes, and even you will think of the past. Think of the one that you promised, that no one should have been on your side. It was a sad lie . . . .

Thus finishes my fantasy; while opening my eyes to the true world, everything has vanished into my dreams, and all that remains is the pain of a jealous love that does not exist any more.

P.S. I trust my faith in what I do. But in fifty-five years it is difficult to remember if the writing in translation is the original one. It is up to the readers' judgement.

Alfredo Cipolato

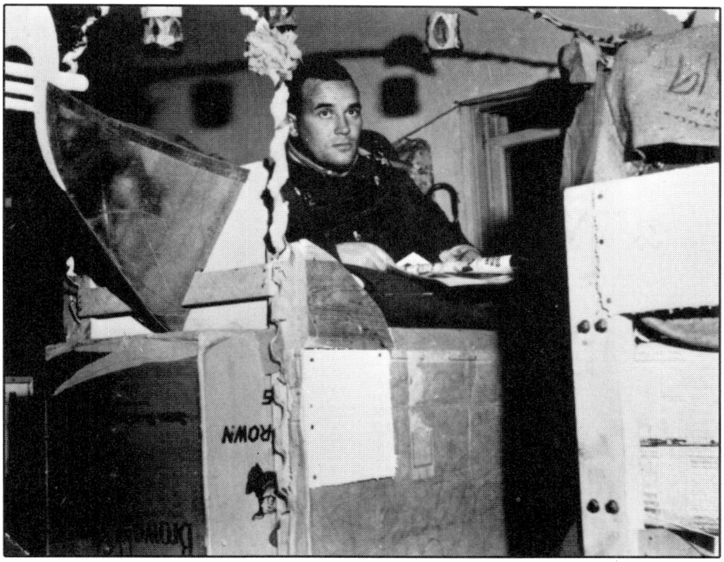

Here is another example of what the Italian internees did at the Fort. In his spare time, Alfredo Cipolato built a gondola. I say that because he had so many activities and responsibilities with the drama group and the light opera group, in addition to his singing. The gondola remained at the Fort, and no one knows what became of it or any of the other artwork. The readers are reminded that the internees in many ways contributed much to this country, as you will see in the following pages.

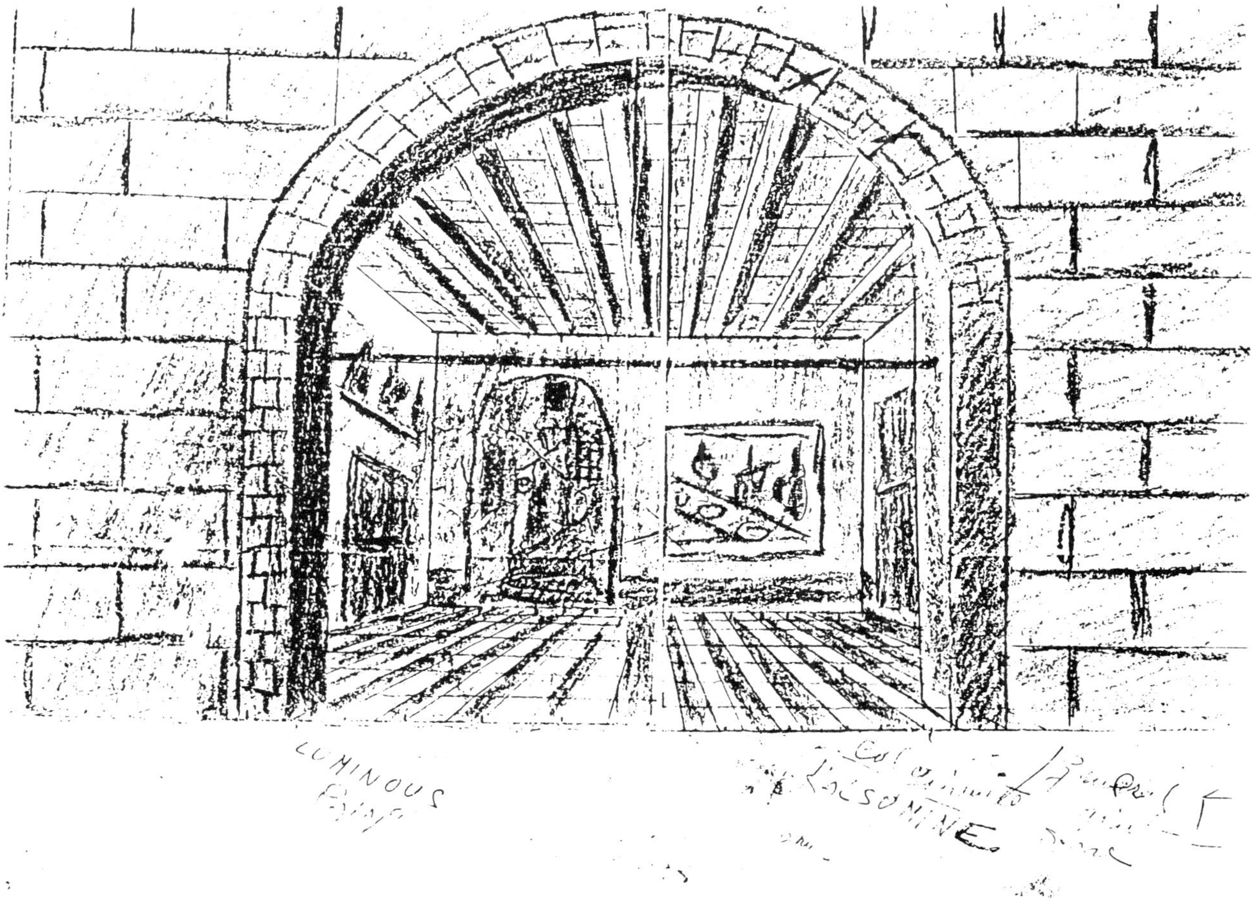

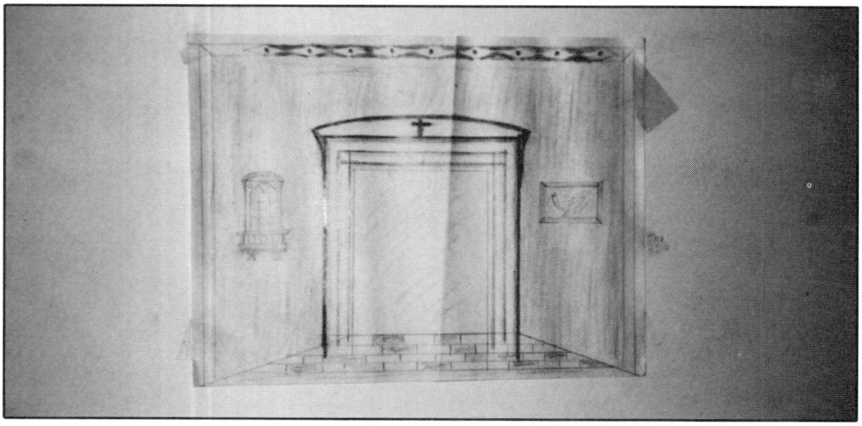

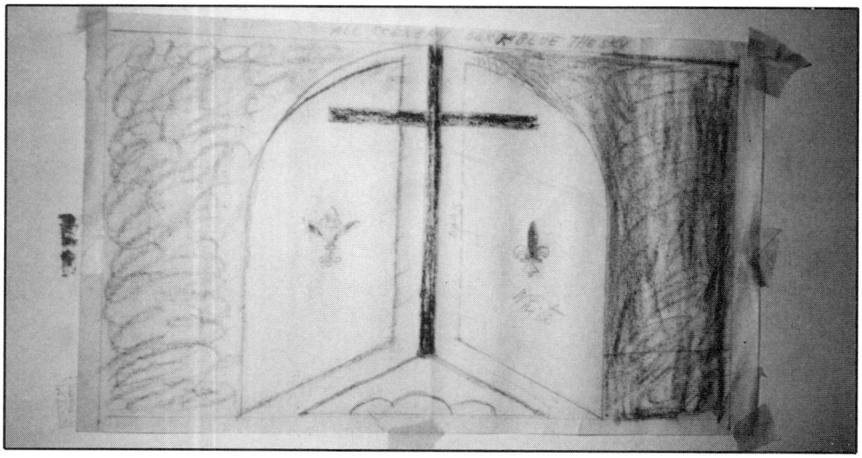

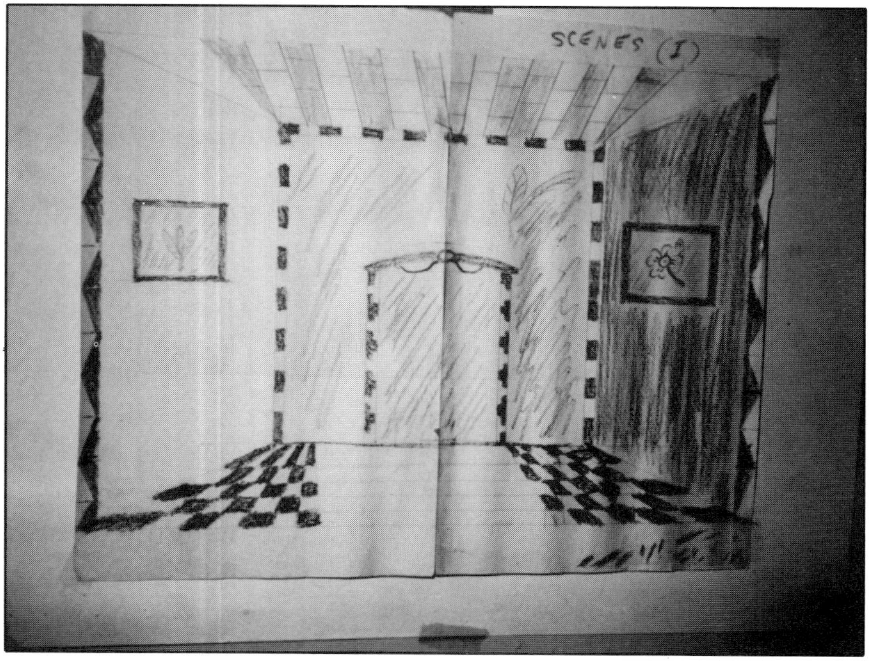
SCENES (I)

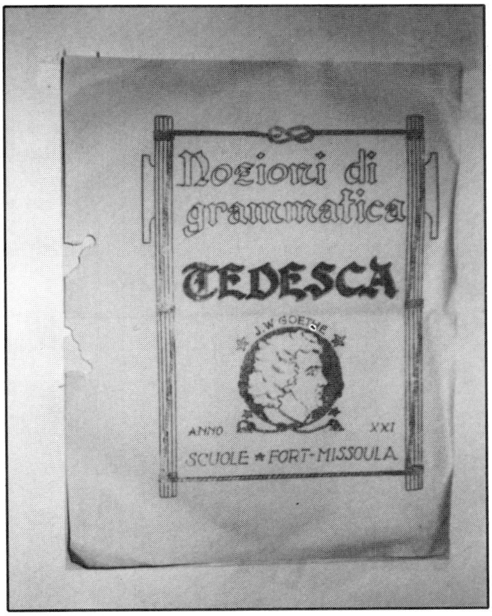
Nozioni di
grammatica
TEDESCA
J.W. GOETHE
ANNO XXI
SCUOLE FORT-MISSOULA

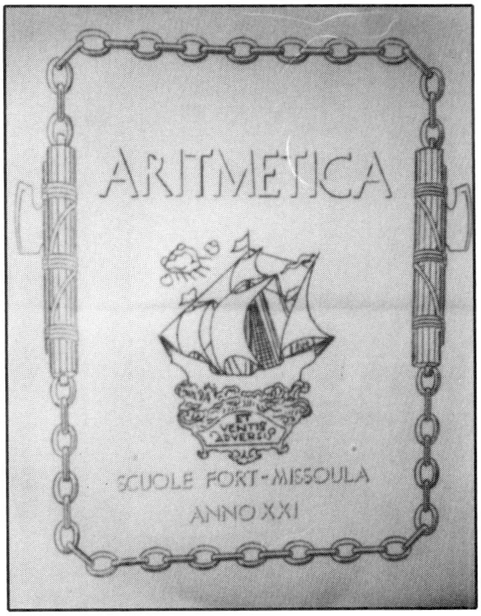
ARITMETICA
SCUOLE FORT-MISSOULA
ANNO XXI

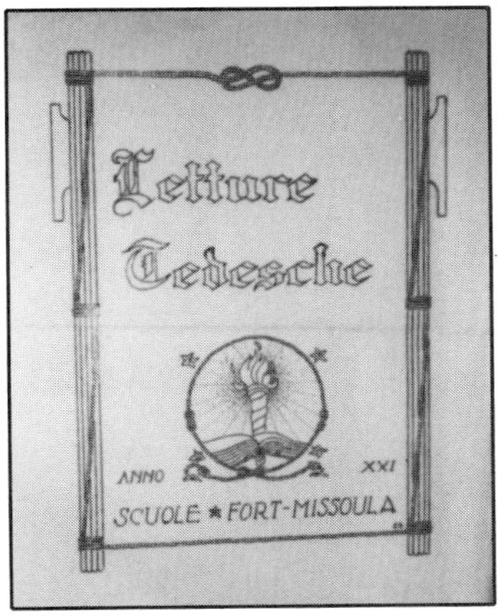
Letture
Tedesche
ANNO XXI
SCUOLE FORT-MISSOULA

These pictures are the covers of books that were created for the Fort school—for example, German grammar, Italian grammar and the maritime book for the 1,200 sailors. The sailors had free choice to study what they wanted. Of course, American language classes were preferred because there were few young boys whose fathers had been in this country before the war. Therefore, they wanted to master the language for their future benefit.

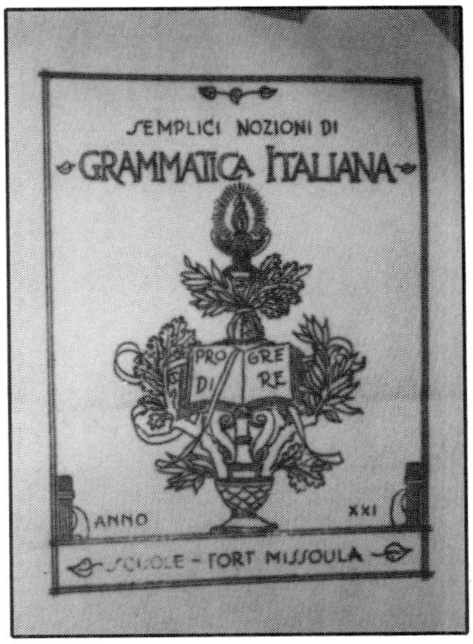
SEMPLICI NOZIONI DI
GRAMMATICA ITALIANA
PRO GRE DI RE
ANNO XXI
SCUOLE - FORT MISSOULA

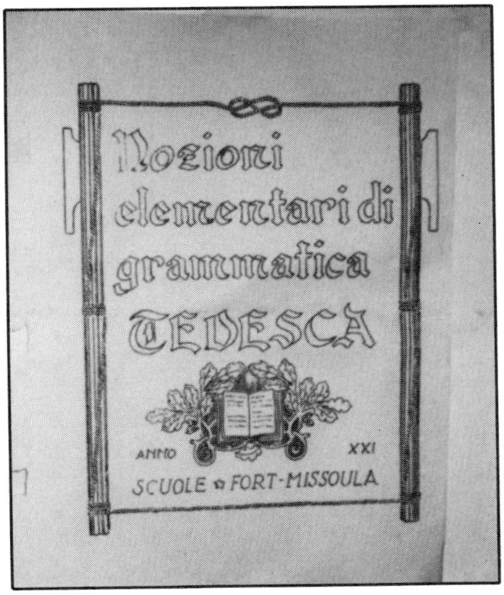
Nozioni
elementari di
grammatica
TEDESCA
ANNO XXI
SCUOLE FORT-MISSOULA

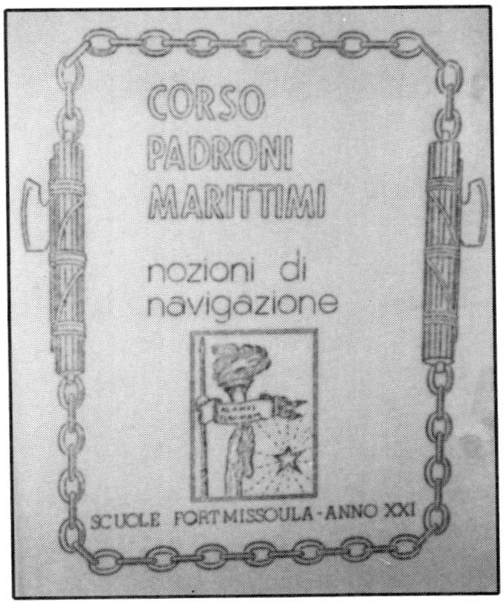
CORSO
PADRONI
MARITTIMI
nozioni di
navigazione
SCUOLE FORTMISSOULA - ANNO XXI

Tools of the Trade

These tools were mine. I used them during navigation when I was with *Il Conte Biancamano* as a cabinetmaker. When I was transferred from the Panama Canal to the United States, I brought them with me to Fort Missoula. These were tools that I used to work during my three years at the Fort. There was a huge, beautiful building that we were so impressed with that later on we used it for theatrical purposes. The large log building in the fort could seat over 800 people. The internees started their own organizations, including an orchestra and a brass band. Others started a theatrical group, putting on plays. With these tools I built a church altar, scenery for the plays that were staged, and used them for many other jobs around the camp including in the carpentry shop. I also built a scaffold when the Ambassador from Switzerland came to Missoula to check our living conditions under the Geneva Convention.

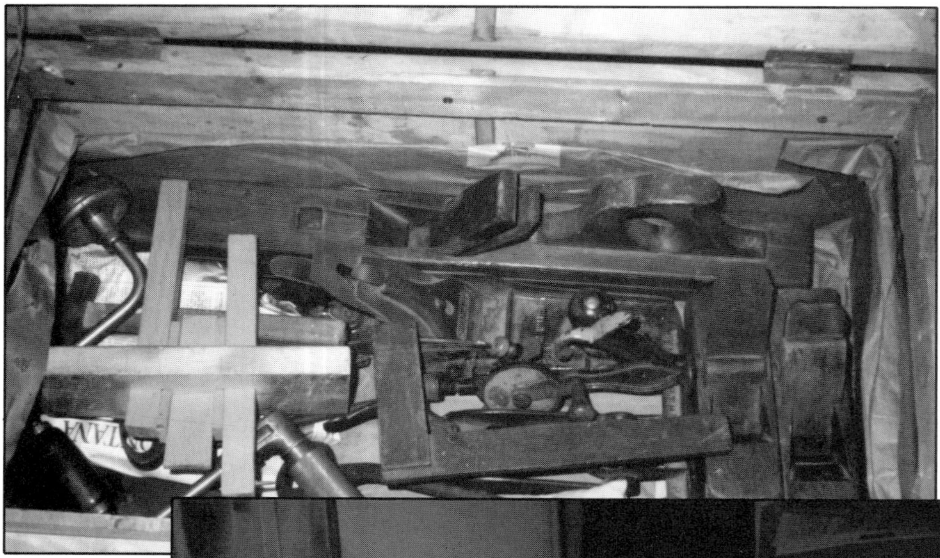

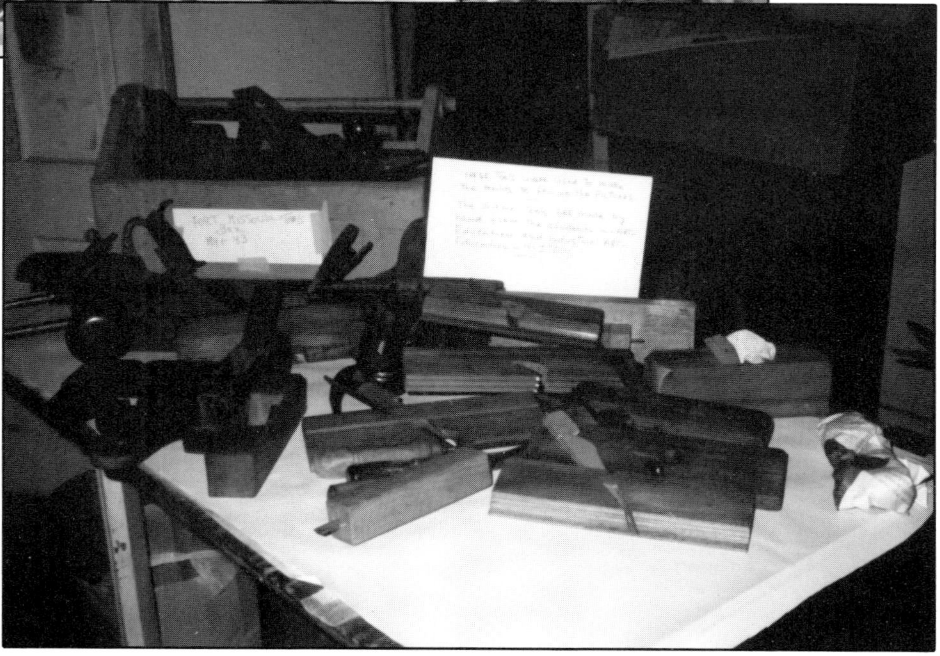

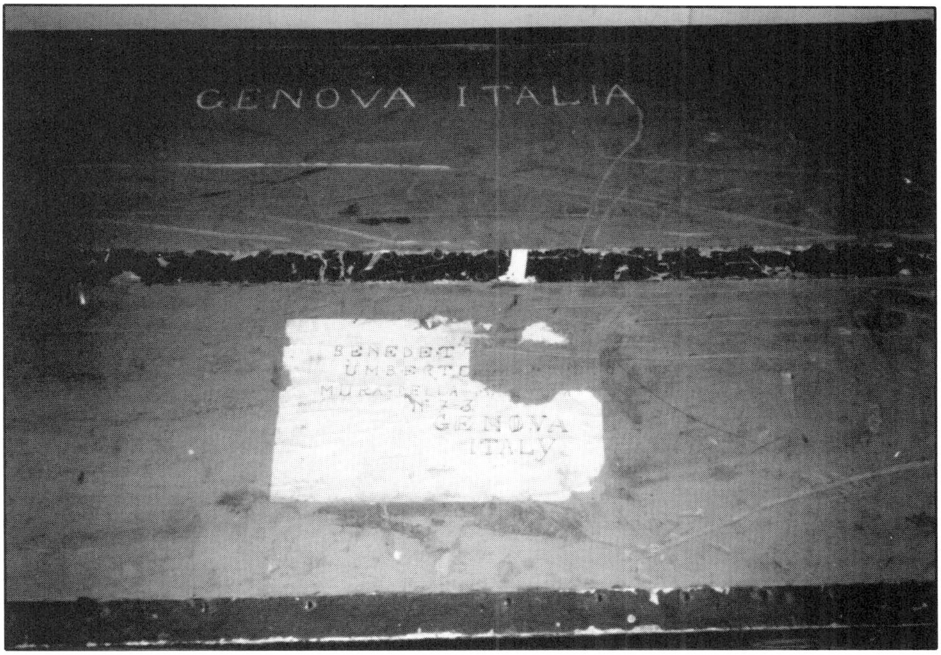
GENOVA ITALIA
GENOVA
ITALY

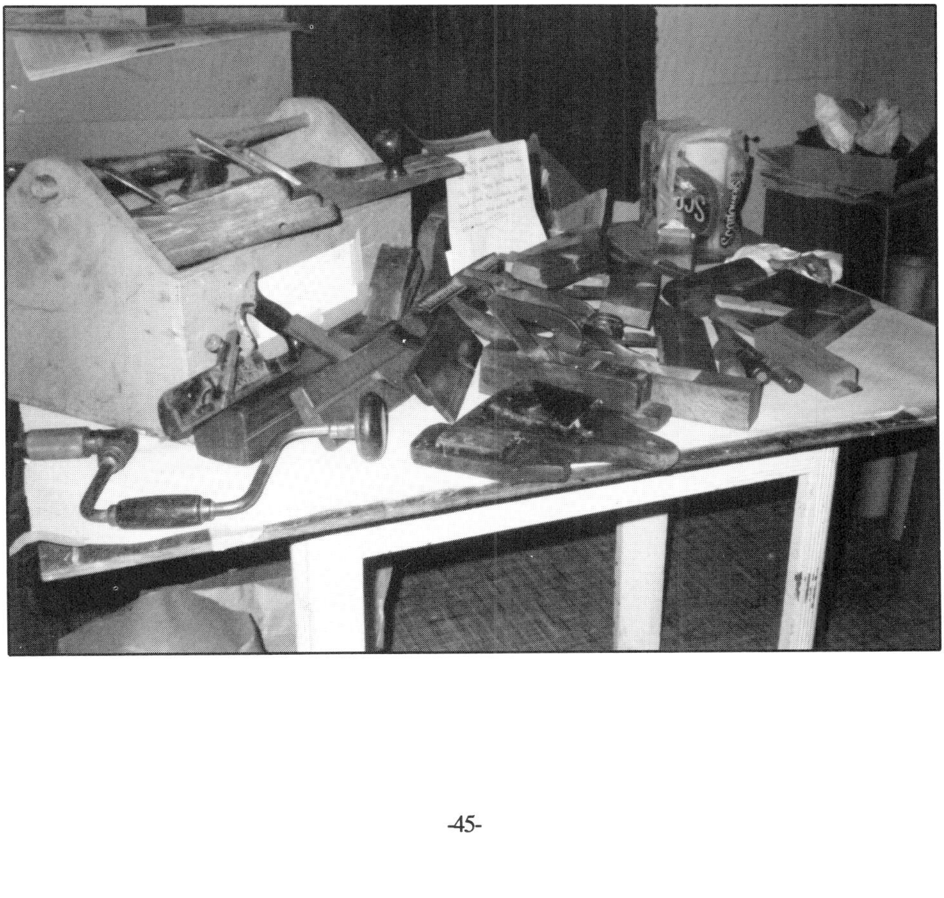

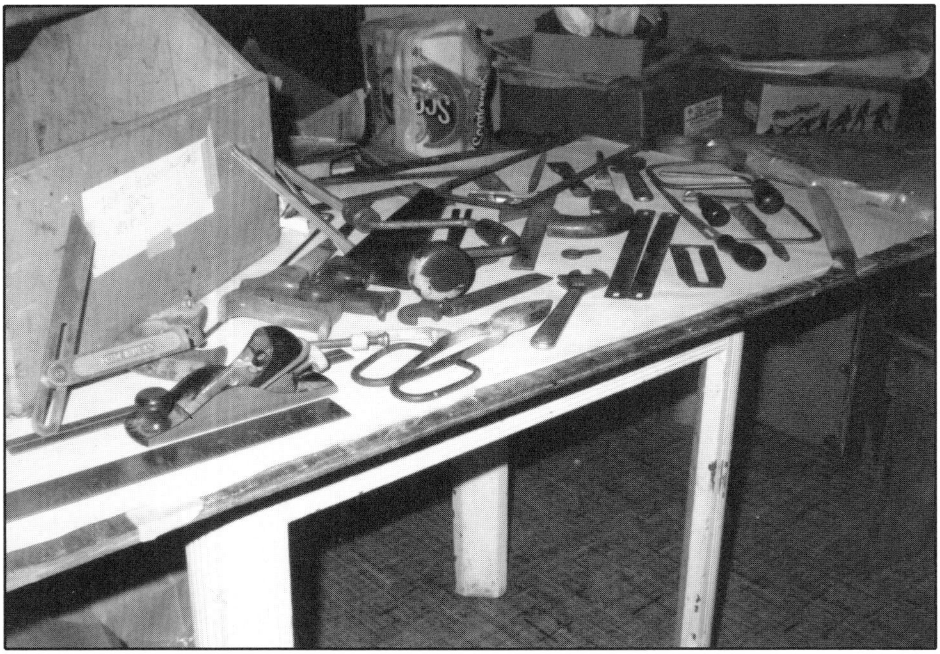

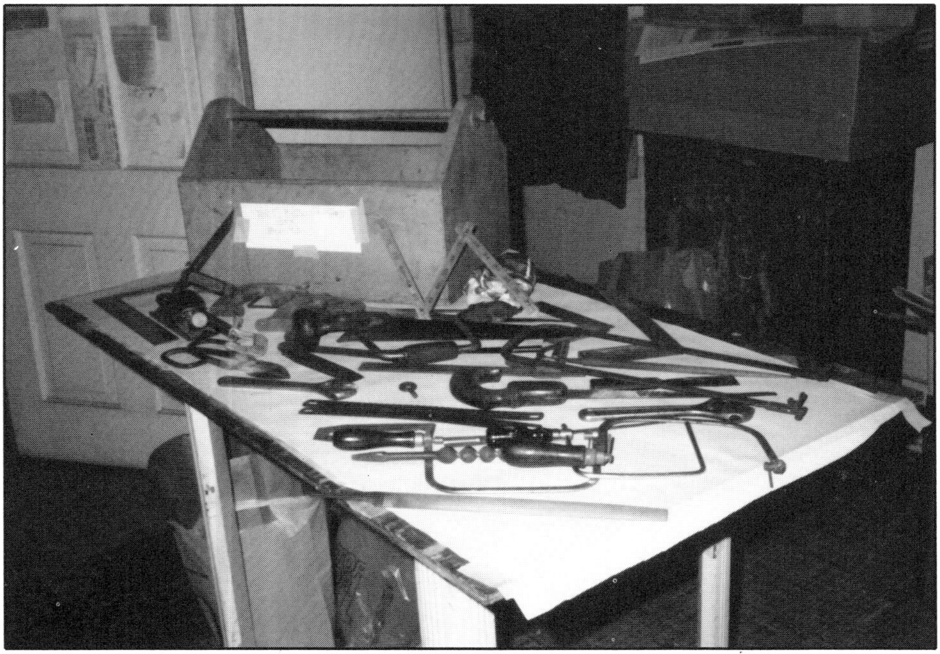

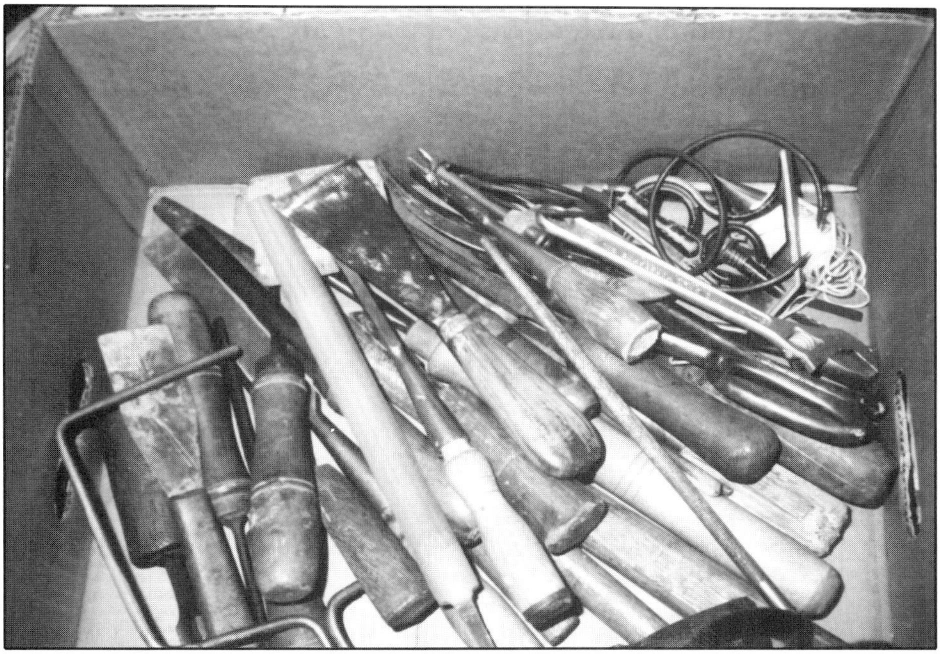

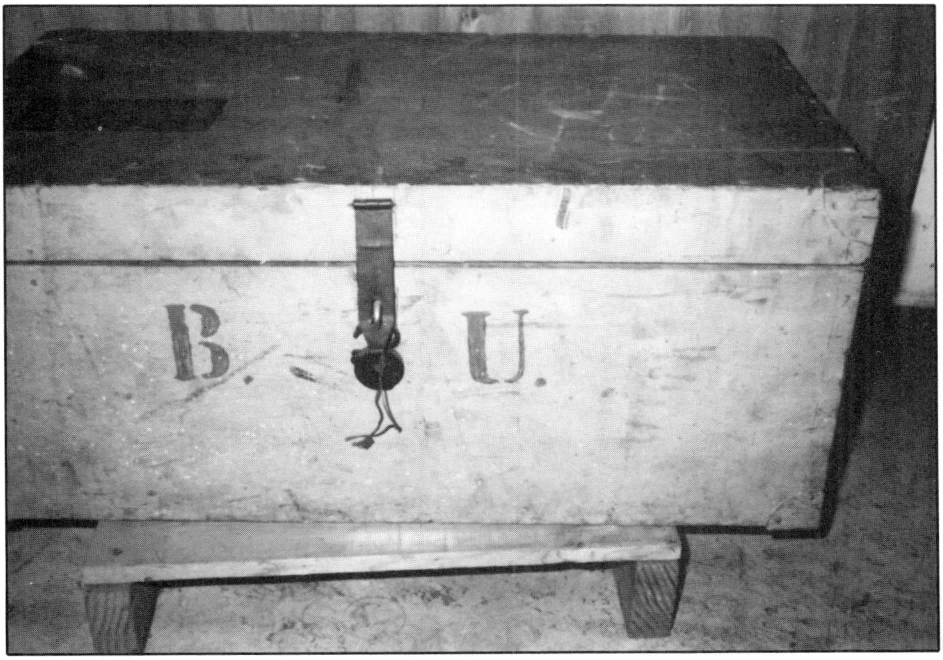
B. U.

Former internees return to barracks

By PATRICIA SULLIVAN
of the Missoulian

Alfredo Cipolato, in "bella voce" under a windy blue sky, sang "O Solo Mio" Monday to commemorate the return of wooden barracks to "Bella Vista," also known as Fort Missoula.

Those barracks served as an internment camp for 1,000 hapless Italians caught in the United States as World War II broke out and for 1,000 Japanese-Americans plucked from their homes on the West Coast and sent inland.

The Historical Museum at Fort Missoula accepted the donation of the 145-by-20-foot barracks from the University of Montana, which needed the land for expansion of its family housing. But it took the Missoula County commissioners and a large number of private businesses, who donated labor and materials, to move the 53-year-old building and set it up at the fort.

Cipolato and Umberto Benedetti, both former internees at Fort Missoula, shared memories of the three years that prisoners were housed there. Benedetti, the first Italian to arrive, recalled that many sailors, used to the sea air, became sick in Montana, "because the climate was very strong." Three died and were buried in the fort's cemetery, he said.

Cipolato, who had worked at the 1940 World's Fair in New York, then at the Fountainbleu Hotel in Miami, recalled how Italian internees were allowed to work outside the camp. He harvested sugar beets for area farmers, worked at St. Patrick Hospital, and labored for the railroad in Missoula. When Missoula's siren sounded, announcing the end of the war, Cipolato said he quit on the spot. But he'd fallen in love with a woman who sang Italian at St. Francis Xavier Church and her father asked him to work in the family store.

The barracks represent "a very significant part of American history and Missoula history," said Robert Brown, director of the historical museum. "It represents a very, very sad period ... but also a period of history we need to remember if it's not to happen again."

The museum plans to use the barracks to house a display of artifacts on the internment camp, to have educational exhibits and to store some unrelated artifacts. The exhibits won't be ready until next spring, but the museum is asking for community help in fixing up the barracks the weekend of April 28-30.

The site of the camp, just east of the historic fort buildings, is on land now owned by The Greens at Fort Missoula, a company that wanted to build a subdivision there. Voters in June 1994 turned down a zoning change that would have allowed the subdivision, but that election is on appeal to the state Supreme Court.

The grass-roots group that opposed the subdivison, Save The Fort Inc. has found barracks from the internment camp in private hands around Missoula, and they have been disassembling and storing them in hopes of getting The Greens property back into public ownership.

Former internees return

Spring 1995 article

Documentation of Immigration

```
                    PASS

BENEDETTI, HUMBERTO, Aline, out and into detention
                    with Recreational Hall
area in connection with carpenter shop activity:

PERMENT UNTIL REVOKED. 5/12/41

                                    _____
                                    Inspector in Charge
                                    Fort Missoula
```

MONTANA HIGHWAY PATROL BOARD
A. F. WINKLER, CHAIRMAN
Motor Vehicle Driver's License
THIS LICENSE MUST BE IN YOUR POSSESSION WHILE OPERATING A MOTOR VEHICLE

N° 15302 -2 CASCADE COUNTY

Name *Umberto Benedetti*
Street _____
City *Gt Falls*

AGE	SEX	WEIGHT	HEIGHT	EYES	HAIR	RACE
32	M	176	5-3	Br	Dk	Cau

License issued this 19 day of June 1944
MICHAEL T. LINNANE, County Treasurer
FEE 75c   By _____

EXPIRES DECEMBER 31, 1944
MOTOR VEHICLE DRIVER'S RECORD

SIGNATURE OF DRIVER
NOT VALID UNLESS SIGNED BY DRIVER TO WHOM THIS LICENSE IS ISSUED

1944

THURBER'S, HELENA

NOTICE OF ALIEN'S ACCEPTABILITY

Date of mailing Sept. 1, 1943

To Benedetti Umberto

Address Columbus Hospital, Great Falls, Mont.

Order No. 2788A

Local Bo[illegible] 93
Missoula County 063
SEP 1 1943 001
Missoula, Montana

(Local board stamp with code)

You are notified that, after considering your status as an alien, the * Army / Navy / Marine Corps has found that you * are, if otherwise qualified, are not acceptable for training and service in the armed forces of the United States.

Marion B. Braj[illegible] Clerk
Member or clerk of local board.

* Strike out portion not applicable.

NOTE

1. If you were found not acceptable to the armed forces, your classification will be changed to Class IV-C.

2. If you were found to be acceptable, your classification will remain unchanged.

D. S. S. Form 307 U. S. GOVERNMENT PRINTING OFFICE 16—26001-1

U. S. DEPARTMENT OF JUSTICE
Immigration and Naturalization Service
Spokane, Washington

May 29, 1943   File No. 9012/7-533

Mr. Umberto Benedetti
c/o Columbus Hospital
Great Falls, Montana

Dear Sir:

      You are informed that the appointment of **Sister Agnes (Mary Dooney)** as sponsor in your case has been approved by this office. In view thereof she will have immediate supervision over your parole and you should consult her for assistance and advice relative to any problems which might arise in connection therewith.

      Under the conditions of your parole you are required to submit reports to this office semi-monthly. You are informed that forms for that purpose have been furnished to your sponsor, who will instruct you in their preparation and also furnish you with whatever assistance may be necessary.

      Owing to the circumstances of your case, you are not exempted from the regulations governing the conduct to be observed by aliens of enemy nationalities. Therefore, you should carefully observe such regulations, a copy of which was furnished you at the time of your release from Fort Missoula.

                            Very truly yours,

                              TOM L. WYCKOFF
                        Acting District Director
                            Spokane District

                By
                      Chief District Parole Officer

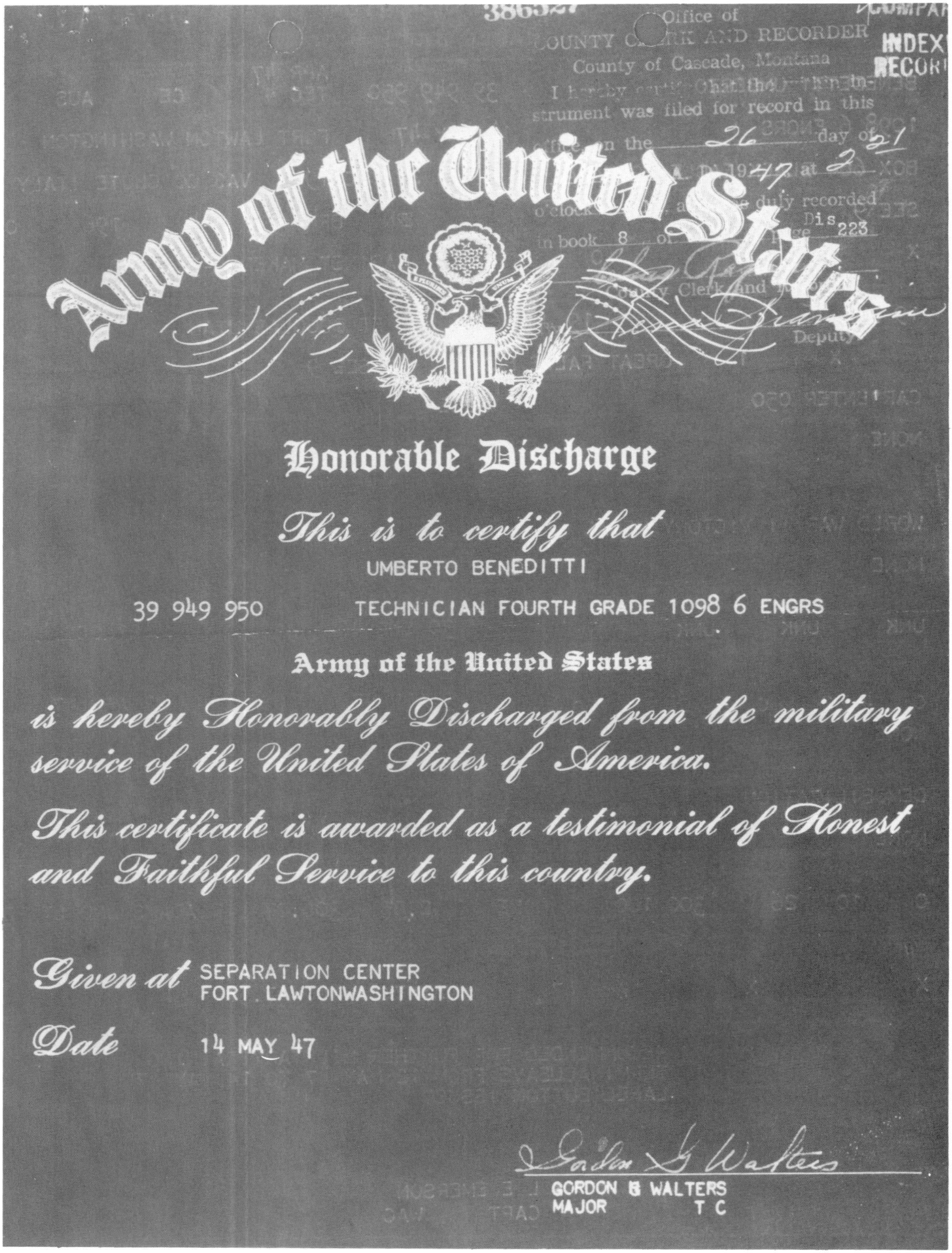

386527

Office of
COUNTY CLERK AND RECORDER
County of Cascade, Montana
I hereby certify that the within instrument was filed for record in this office on the 26 day of 21 A.D. 1947 at 2 o'clock and duly recorded in book 8 of Dis page 223

County Clerk and Recorder

Deputy

INDEX
RECORD

Army of the United States

Honorable Discharge

This is to certify that

UMBERTO BENEDITTI

39 949 950 TECHNICIAN FOURTH GRADE 1098 6 ENGRS

Army of the United States

is hereby Honorably Discharged from the military service of the United States of America.

This certificate is awarded as a testimonial of Honest and Faithful Service to this country.

Given at SEPARATION CENTER
FORT LAWTONWASHINGTON

Date 14 MAY 47

GORDON G WALTERS
MAJOR T C

MRID Form No. 22
Rev 29 Nov 1945

MEAL TICKET

Number

Date JUNE

Good Only At
MOXOM CAFE
34 W. Broadway Butte, Mont.

Value
ONE (1) MEAL
will be furnished bearer on presentation of this ticket

Signature of Issuing Officer

H. C. McKNIGHT, Major, AUS
Purchasing & Contracting Officer
Mont. Dist. Mil. Pers. Proc. Sv.
321 W. Galena St., Butte, Mont.

Signature of Applicant

P. X. 6th Engr
Coca Cola

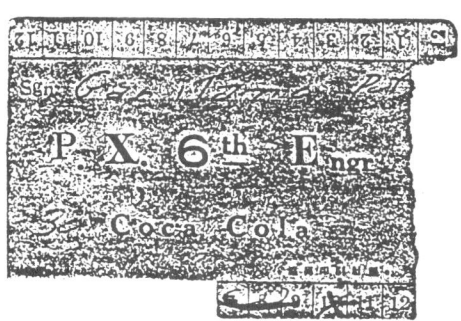

Co. "B", 1st Replacement Depot
This ticket entitles the bearer to eat evening meal.

GROVER E. NASH
Capt., FA
Commanding.

U.S.S. GENERAL H. B. FREEMAN
Meal Ticket No. 9U
Voyage No.
Name

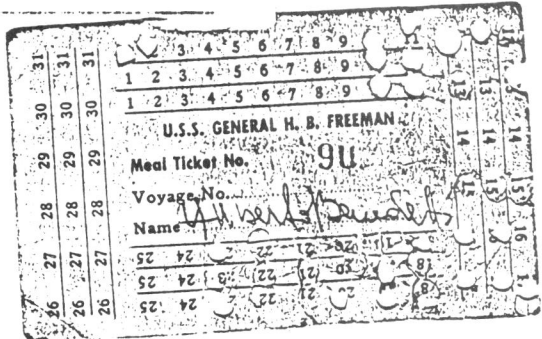

Remembering the Trips

Strange as it may be, Mr. Umberto Benedetti went from being an internee at Fort Missoula, Montana, to being on a transport boat from Oakland, California, to South Korea.

Two boats were reactivated for transportation of troops, without taking into consideration that the Pacific Ocean is different from other oceans—the waves do not break, but rather roll. From Oakland, California, to South Korea it took 24 days, with a stop in the Hawaiian Islands. In comparison, coming back on the *General H.B. Freeman* it took only 18 days from South Korea to Seattle, Washington. This section presents remembrances of the joy and fun that Mr. Benedetti had with the troops during all their activities and voyages.

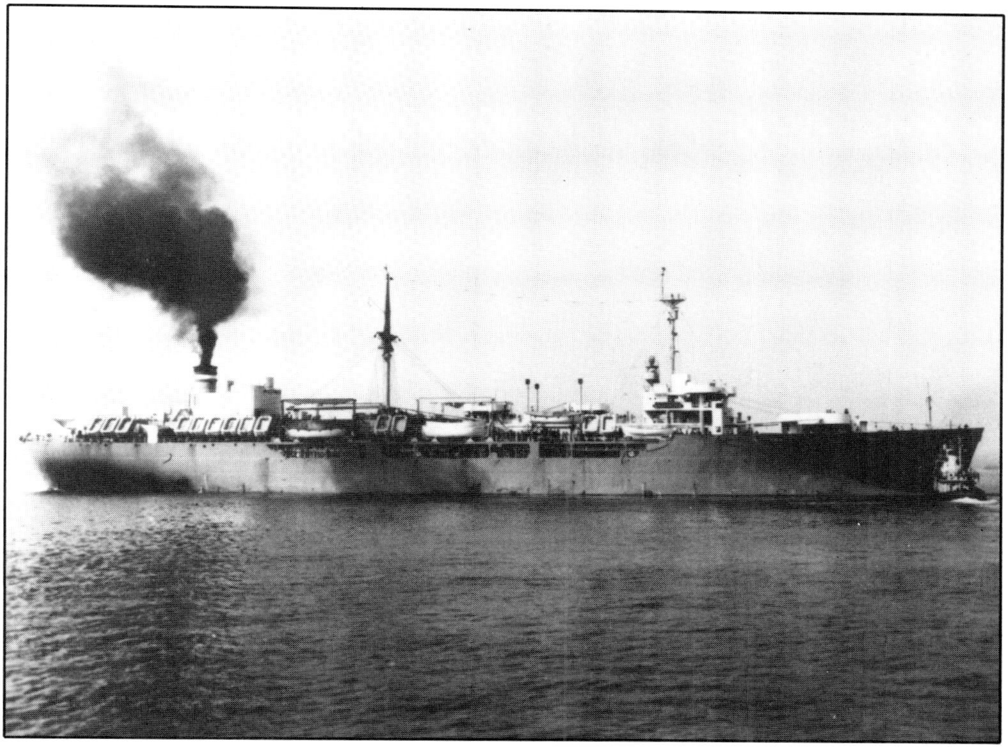

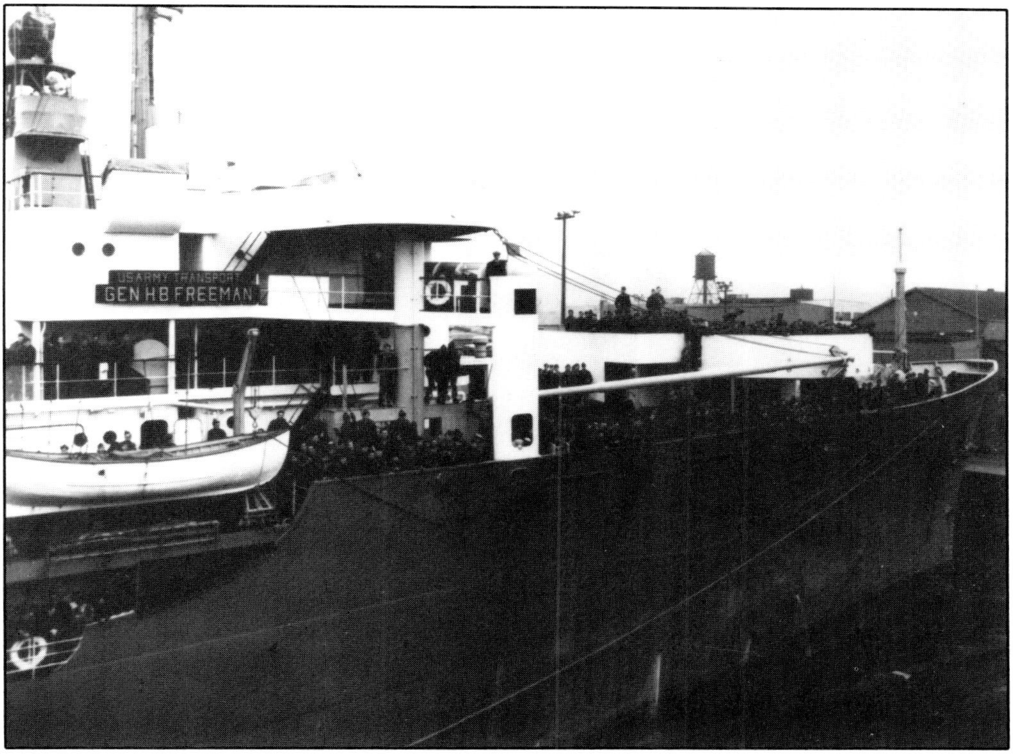
US ARMY TRANSPORT
GEN H B FREEMAN

111

RATION CARD
ARMY EXCHANGE SERVICE, KOREA

BRANCH EXCHANGE No. _____

NAME: **Benedetti Umberto**

ASN: 39949915 GRADE: T/5 ORGANIZATION: H&S Co 6th Engr C Bn

APPROVED SIGNATURE _____
BRANCH EXCHANGE OFFICER

RATION PERIOD AND ALLOWANCE AS POSTED
COUPONS VOID IF DETACHED FROM CARD

Tobacco	Soap	Special	Candy
	M M	x-13	
	L L	x-12	
	K K	x-11	
J	J J	x-10	10
I	I I	x-9	9
H	H H	x-8	8
G	G G	x-7	7
F	F F	x-6	6
E	E E	x-5	5
D	D D	x-4	4
C	C C	x-3	3
B	B B	x-2	2
A	A A	x-1	1

HEADQUARTERS 5TH ENGINEER COMBAT BATTALION
APO 6

TEMPORARY PASS

Umberto, Benedetti Pfc. 39949950 H & S Co.
Name   Rank   ASN   Organization

is authorized to be absent from their organization for the purpose of:

visiting Paris, France

From 1800 7 Dec 46
To 2300 14 Dec

_____   _____   John D Hogue
Violation   Place   (CO Signature)
                                Capt.
_____   _____   (Title & Grade)
Date   Time
                                _____
                                (Organization)

HQS COMPANY, 6TH ENGINEER COMBAT BATTALION
APO 6

Umberto Benedetti   T5   39949950   1098th EUD.
Name   Rank   ASN   Organization

is authorized to be absent from their organization for the purpose of:

From 1600
To   2400

Villatto 24   _____   _____
Jan. 25 47   PLACE   CO Signature
                          Major C.E.
_____   _____   Title & Grade
Date   Time   1098th EUD.
                          Organization

OFFICE OF THE POST ENGINEER
CAMP PUSAN

24 JANUARY 1947

THE FOLLOWING NAMED ENLISTED MEN OF THE 1098TH E.U.D.,
ARE AUTHORIZED TO VISIT H&S CO. BARBER SHOP, BETWEEN THE
HOURS OF 0800 AND 1700, 24 JAN. 1947.

T/5 BENEDETTI,
PFC TANEZ

Howard J. Elliott
HOWARD J. ELLIOTT
CAPTAIN, CORPS OF ENG.
ASST. POST ENG.

OFFICE OF THE POST ENGINEER,
CAMP PUSAN
APO 6

30 January, 1947

To Whom it May Concern:

T/5 Benedetti, 1098th Eng. Util. Detach. has permission of this office to visit shower room between the hours of 1600 and 1700, this date.

Howard J. Elliott
HOWARD J. ELLIOTT,
Capt. Corps of Engineers
Asst. Post Engineer.

OFFICE OF THE SURGEON
1ST REPLACEMENT BATTALION
APO 815

APR 6 1945

CERTIFICATE OF HEALTH

DATE_____

NAME UMBERTO BENEDETTI   RANK T/4   ASN 39949950

    1. This is to certify the above named individual was inspected this date and found free from vermin and quarantinable diseases. Immunizations required by War Department or the Directives have been completed and noted on WD AGO Form 8-177, Immunization register. (Or WD Form 81, US Army.)

    2. Exceptions to the above are....................................
....
....

    3. The following are the unusual or significant infections and parasitic diseases and vermin infections to which this individual may have been exposed. These and other deficiencies, for full satisfaction of War Department requirements will be brought to the attention of Surgeons in ports or airports of destination.
....
....
....

LEO D. KLAUBER
1st Lt. MC
Depot Surgeon

    The bearer of this pass is authorized to be absent from his organization in fatigues as he is member of an emergency work crew for the Post Engineer.

E A VITT
Major CE
Post Engineer

Form I-220.
UNITED STATES DEPARTMENT OF JUSTICE
IMMIGRATION AND NATURALIZATION SERVICE
(Edition 5-15-45)

ORDER OF PAROLE

District No. __10__

Alien No. __A-5960233__

In the case of __UMBERTO BENEDETTI__

a citizen of __Italy__ who has been excluded from admission into the United States or arrested in deportation proceedings.

It appearing that said alien may be paroled under the supervision of the Immigration and Naturalization Service as provided in Operations Instruction 150.5 I, IT IS HEREBY ORDERED that such alien be paroled and permitted to be and remain at large during compliance with the following conditions:

(a) That said subject shall report to the sponsor named on the reverse hereof as specified in paragraph (e);

(b) That said subject shall report to the designated parole officer of this Service as specified in paragraph (f);

(c) That said subject shall notify the designated parole officer of this Service of any change in residence or employment within an Immigration and Naturalization Service district within 48 hours after change is made;

(d) That said subject shall not change his residence or employment from one Immigration and Naturalization Service district to any place outside thereof without prior knowledge of the designated parole officer of this Service;

(e) That said subject shall report to his sponsor weekly;

(f) That said subject shall report to the District Director, Immigration and Naturalization Service, Spokane, Wash., on the first of each month, by letter.

This order shall be vacated and set aside upon the cancellation of the immigration proceedings.

DATE: August 15, 1947

D. W. BREWSTER (Signature of District Director) District Director

(OVER)

I, UMBERTO BENEDETTI, hereby acknowledge that I have read and understand the conditions of my parole as set forth in this order; I further understand that failure to comply with said conditions will constitute sufficient cause for the revocation of my parole; I hereby affirm and agree that I will abide by the said conditions; and I further agree to appear voluntarily when instructed to do so by an officer of the Immigration and Naturalization Service.

Umberto Benedetti
(Parolee)
St. Thomas Orphans' Home
Great Falls, Montana
(Address)

Subscribed before me at Great Falls, Montana this 15th day of August, 1947

Lars C. Larson
Immigrant Inspector
(Title)

I, Sister Mary Evelyn, Superior, hereby acknowledge that I understand the conditions hereinabove set forth and hereby agree to furnish written reports to the designated Parole Officer concerning the subject alien's conduct and activities; and, further, that I will immediately report to the designated Parole Officer any failure on the part of the said subject alien to comply with the conditions of parole or any fact coming to my attention which would indicate that the subject alien intends to abscond or otherwise violate the conditions of parole.

Sister Mary Evelyn
(Sponsor)

St. Thomas Orphans' Home
Great Falls, Montana
(Address)

DATE: August 15, 1947

16—44779-1   U. S. GOVERNMENT PRINTING OFFICE

"My Heart Tells Me"

My heart tells me this is just a fling
yet you say that love means everything.
Do you mean what you are saying?
Or is this a little game you are playing?

My heart tells me I will cry again,
lips that kiss like yours will lie again?
Am I fool enough to see it through?
Will I be sorry if I do?
Will I believe my heart—or you?

****

Some of these poems and other translations were written in the period of the 1940s in the detention camp, as free thoughts of personal expression, without thinking about the art of writing.

THE WHITE HOUSE

WASHINGTON, DC APR 26 1977 PM

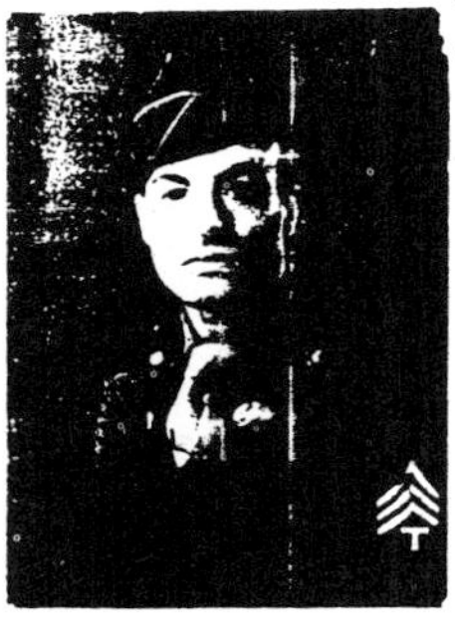

FROM
THE WHITE HOUSE
WASHINGTON, D.C.

Mr. Umberto Benedetti
c/o The Printing Services
The University of Montana
Missoula, Montana 59801

THE WHITE HOUSE
WASHINGTON

President and Mrs. Carter regret that their official duties preclude their responding to the large number of special requests that they receive. We hope that you will understand.

STAFF ASSISTANT

COMRADES

IN ORDER TO HONOR MY HONEST ACCOMPLISHMENT, YOU MAY DISPLAY THIS ENVELOPE FROM THE WHITE HOUSE DOCUMENTING MY BOOK, A CULTURAL FREEDOM OF PRESS. ALSO MY PICTURE AND THE EMBLEM OF BROKEN WING I RECEIVED AS AN HONOR FOR MILITARY SERVICE DURING THE SECOND WORLD WAR AND THE KOREAN CONFLICT. I DEEPLY APPRECIATE YOUR CONSIDERATION OF AN "OLD VETERAN". THANK YOU.

UMBERTO BENEDETTI

The Historical Museum at Fort Missoula

This is the Historical Museum today. If a visitor were to look around, they would see the beauty of Missoula's spectacular valley.

The valley is surrounded by mountains as far as the eye can see. The mountains offer some protection from the elements to the City of Missoula and nearby valley towns.

Montana has much beauty to be appreciated and is truly a "Treasure State."

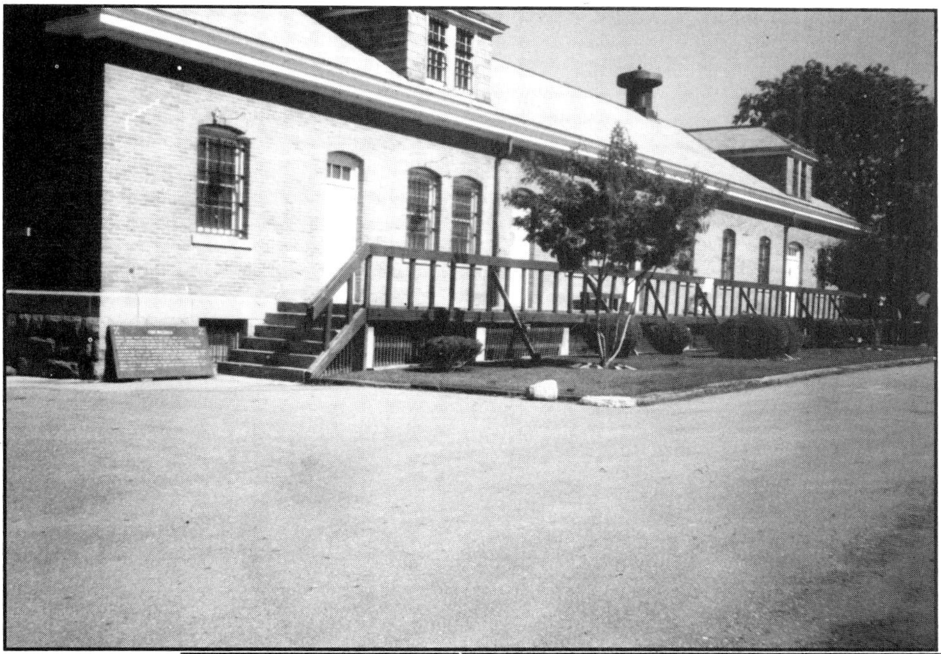

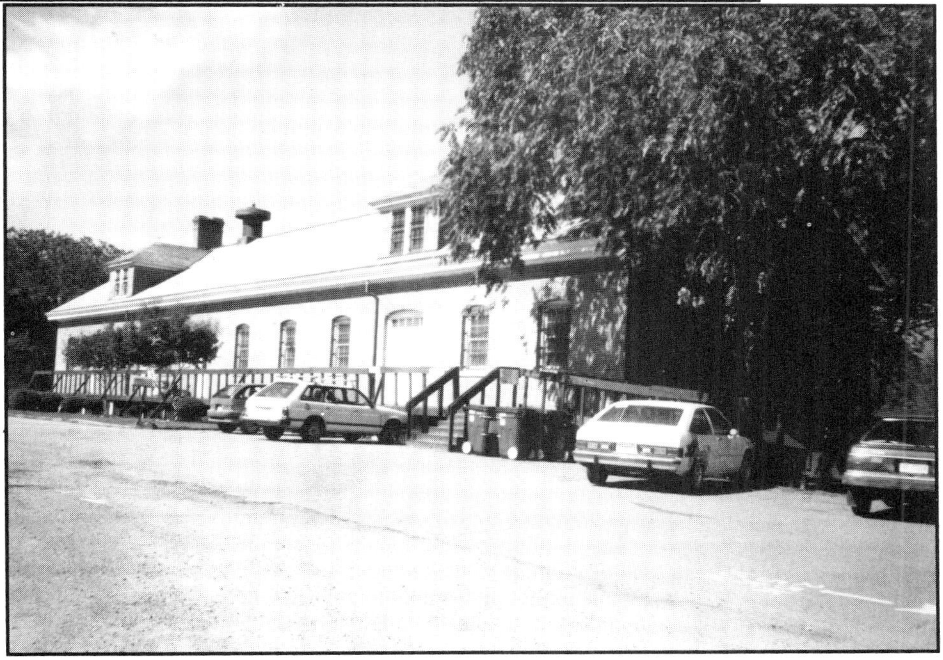

Raymond Visciano
A True Story of a Fort Missoula Boy

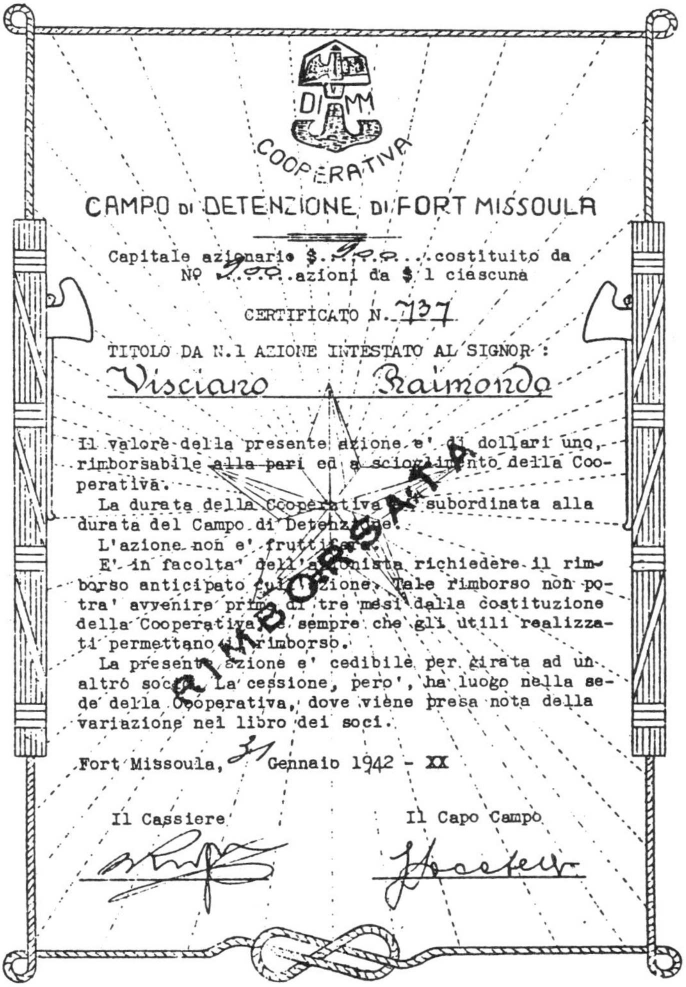
COOPERATIVA

CAMPO DI DETENZIONE DI FORT MISSOULA

Capitale azionario $. 900 . . . costituito da
Nº 900 azioni da $ 1 ciascuna

CERTIFICATO N. 737

TITOLO DA N.1 AZIONE INTESTATO AL SIGNOR :
Visciano Raimondo

Il valore della presente azione e' di dollari uno, rimborsabile ~~alla pari~~ ed a scioglimento della Cooperativa.

La durata della Cooperativa e' subordinata alla durata del Campo di Detenzione.

L'azione non e' fruttifera.

E' in facolta' dell'azionista richiedere il rimborso anticipato dell'azione. Tale rimborso non potra' avvenire prima di tre mesi dalla costituzione della Cooperativa, e sempre che gli utili realizzati permettano il rimborso.

La presente azione e' cedibile per girata ad un altro socio. La cessione, pero', ha luogo nella sede della Cooperativa, dove viene presa nota della variazione nel libro dei soci.

Fort Missoula, 31 Gennaio 1942 - XX

Il Cassiere | Il Capo Campo

RIMBORSATA

This memo shows the readers that Visciano Raimondo purchased some items for the cooperative. It was like the military PX system that we have in the United States.

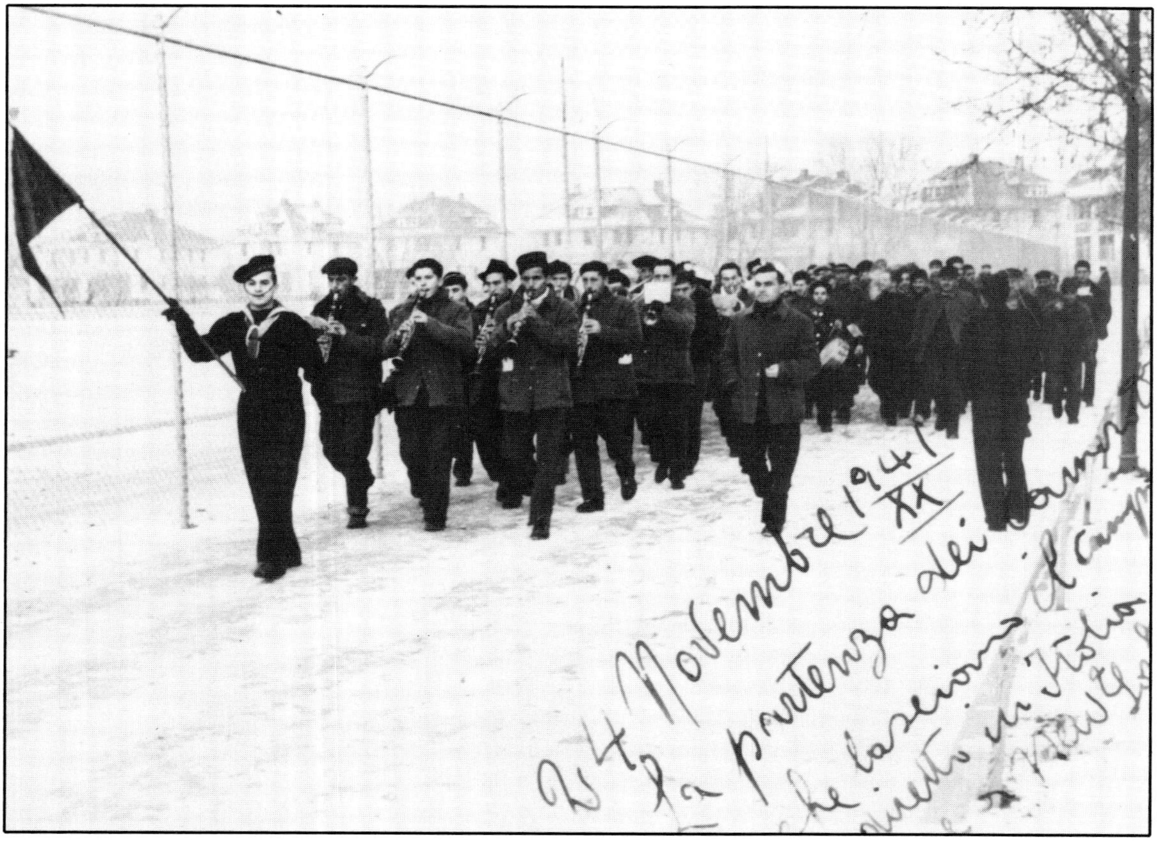
24 Novembre 1941
XX
la partenza dei

Italians marching along the compounds fence in November 1941. Visciano Raimondo is carrying the "Gagliardetto," the penant flag. The houses in the background are the officer's quarters of Fort Missoula. The Italians were the first to organize all kinds of activities in order to keep the internees busy so they would not dwell on the course of the war.

To the Readers:

Many have written their own story about Fort Missoula during World War II. The story that you are reading is a true story, illustrated with black and white photographs that were taken during the period, showing the contributions that the "boys of Fort Missoula" did during and after the War.

Raimondo Visciano, from Torre del Greco (Naples), Italy, began working aboard the *SS Belvedere*, owned by a company in Genova, Italy. In June 1940, the *Belvedere* was anchored in Philadelphia, Pennsylvania, waiting there with hopes that the political situation would get better. However, while they were staying in American waters the situation became worse. Therefore, the crew of the *Belvedere*, seeing that hope was lost, went to night school in order to learn more of the English language. Meanwhile, Raimondo was registered by the Selective Service System, as many other boys were. In December 1940, Visciano's number was called for military service. But since he was aboard an alien ship, he was released by the Selective Service.

In March 1941, the crew of the *Belvedere* along with personnel from the New York World's Fair were picked up by the Immigration and Naturalization Service and shipped to Fort Missoula, Montana. The story of Visciano does not finish at the Fort. When he was released from the camp, he worked in Frenchtown, Montana, from 1942 to 1943. In December 1943, he went to work at Columbus Hospital in Great Falls, Montana, as an orderly. Again, to illustrate to the readers how the government worked in time of war, Raimondo was drafted for a short period of time in December 1944. As a strange coincidence, in 1949, when he was in New York, Raimondo took a job as a Medical Technician on the U.S. Army hospital ship *Mercy*. In 1950, he was again called to work on the *Mercy*, and decided to make a career in the Army. He spent 20 years in the service as a Radiological (X-Ray) Technician.

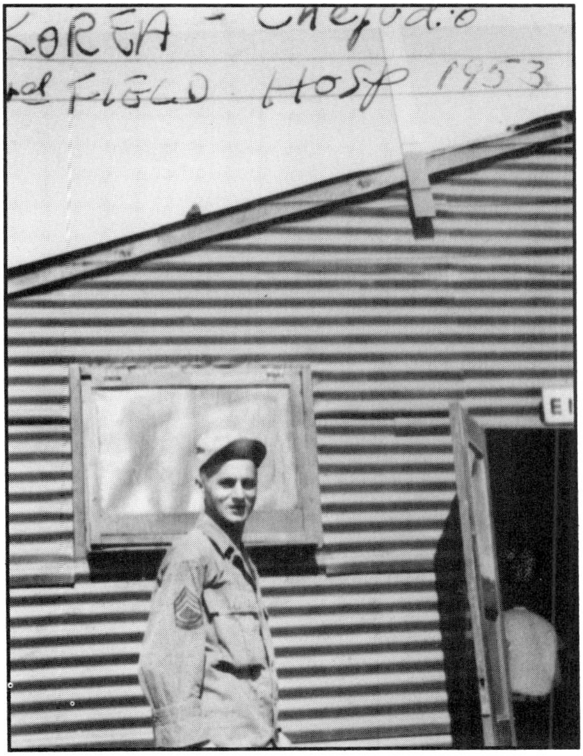
KOREA -
FIELD HOSP 1953

Going back to New York in 1966, Raimondo found a job at the Catholic Hospital "Mercy" on Long Island. Finally, in January 1980, he decided to go to Florida, where he is still living with his wife, whom he met while in the Army. And that is a short story of one of the Fort Missoula "boys."

Some writers are confused over whether they were "incarcerated" or were "prisoners." A better description is that these young men were "interned" in a relocation camp, awaiting their release by the Immigration and Naturalization Service.

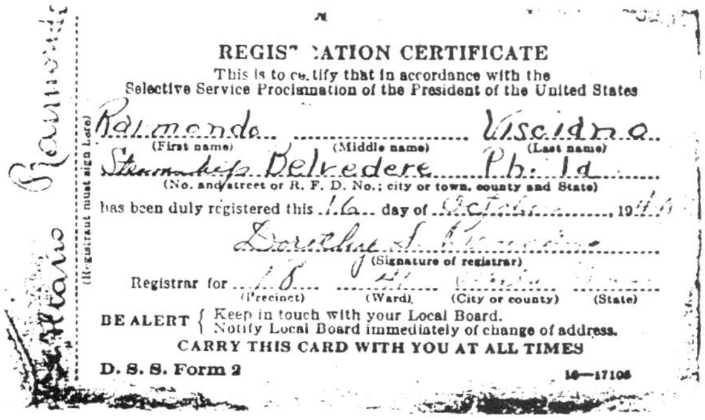

REGIS' :ATION CERTIFICATE
This is to certify that in accordance with the Selective Service Proclamation of the President of the United States

Raimondo .... Visciano
(First name) (Middle name) (Last name)
Steamship Belvedere Phila
(No. and street or R. F. D. No.; city or town, county and State)
has been duly registered this 16 day of October, 1944
Dorothy S. ...
(Signature of registrar)
Registrar for 18 ...
(Precinct) (Ward) (City or county) (State)

BE ALERT { Keep in touch with your Local Board. Notify Local Board immediately of change of address.
CARRY THIS CARD WITH YOU AT ALL TIMES
D. S. S. Form 2 16—17105

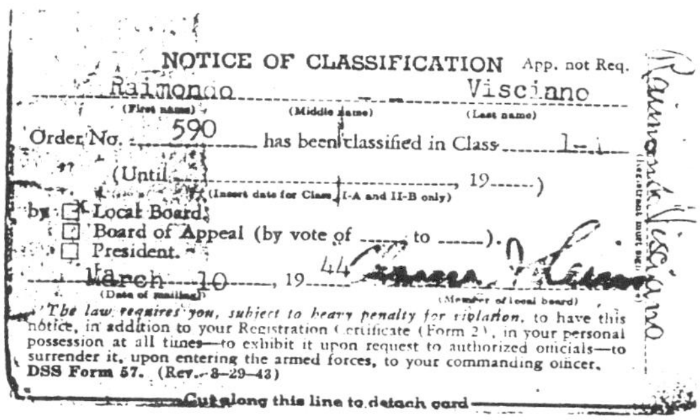

NOTICE OF CLASSIFICATION App. not Req.
Raimondo Visciano
(First name) (Middle name) (Last name)
Order No. 590 has been classified in Class 1-A
(Until ...., 19......)
(Insert date for Class I-A and II-B only)
by ☒ Local Board.
☐ Board of Appeal (by vote of ...... to ......).
☐ President.
March 10, 1944
(Date of mailing) (Member of local board)
The law requires you, subject to heavy penalty for violation, to have this notice, in addition to your Registration Certificate (Form 2), in your personal possession at all times—to exhibit it upon request to authorized officials—to surrender it, upon entering the armed forces, to your commanding officer.
DSS Form 57. (Rev. 3-29-43)
Cut along this line to detach card

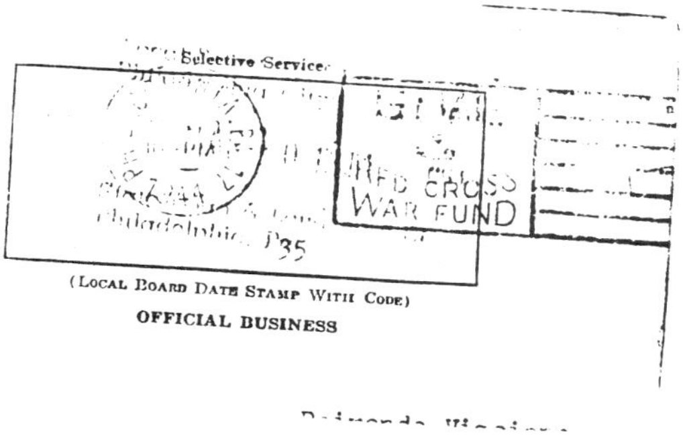

Selective Service
RED CROSS WAR FUND
Philadelphia P35
(Local Board Date Stamp With Code)
OFFICIAL BUSINESS

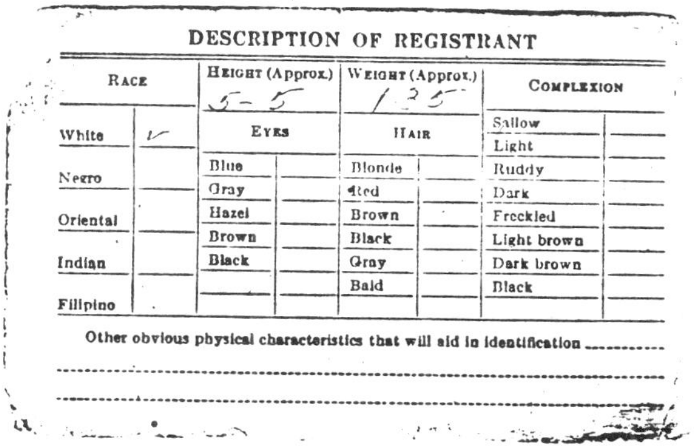

DESCRIPTION OF REGISTRANT

Race		Height (Approx.)		Weight (Approx.)		Complexion	
		5-5		135			
White	✓	Eyes		Hair		Sallow	
						Light	
Negro		Blue		Blonde		Ruddy	
		Gray		Red		Dark	
Oriental		Hazel		Brown		Freckled	
		Brown		Black		Light brown	
Indian		Black		Gray		Dark brown	
				Bald		Black	
Filipino							

Other obvious physical characteristics that will aid in identification ....

Raimondo Visciano
Identification Cards from the Selective Service

HEADQUARTERS
KOREAN COMMUNICATIONS ZONE
APO 234

C I T A T I O N

COMMENDATION RIBBON WITH METAL PENDANT

Sergeant First Class RAIMONDO VISCIANO, RA39938097, Army Medical Service, United States Army. Sergeant VISCIANO, a member of 3rd Field Hospital, is cited for meritorious service in Korea during the period 4 January to 31 August 1953. As Chief X-ray Technician he established the finest X-ray section in the area, expertly trained replacement personnel to perform section functions and effectively assisted in improving the appearance of the hospital grounds. Sergeant VISCIANO performed the many duties attendant to his position in a highly exemplary manner and contributed materially to the success achieved by his organization in accomplishing its vital mission. The meritorious service rendered by Sergeant VISCIANO throughout this period reflects great credit on himself and the military service.

OFFICIAL:

C. E. WELCH
CWO   USA
Asst AG

(GO 222, 22 Sep 53)

PATTERSON ARMY HOSPITAL
Fort Monmouth, New Jersey

SIGFM/SU 201   19 May 1958

SUBJECT: Letter of Appreciation

THRU: Troop Commander
        Hospital Detachment (61-1301-1)
        Patterson Army Hospital
        Fort Monmouth, New Jersey

TO: SFC Raimondo Visciano
        RA 39 938 097
        Hospital Detachment (61-1301-1)
        Patterson Army Hospital
        Fort Monmouth, New Jersey

   A visitor talked with me Saturday afternoon after touring the hospital. In his conversation he used two phrases; "espirit de corps" and "high morale". It was only after this that he remarked about the facilities of the new hospital.

   It was your presence, action and words, when combined with the members of the team, that produced this reaction.

   It is for this, I wish to extend my appreciation to you. You have been a soldier and served in your position with credit.

   Let this be a reminder to us all that every visitor in the hospital even if seeking medical care or visiting a hospitalized friend can be pleased.

                                        S. E. VOSBURGH
                                        Major, MSC
                                        Co-ordinator, Armed Forces
                                        Day Activity

28 June 65

~~SP5~~ SFC Raimondo Visciano
Radiology Service
Valley Forge General Hospital
Phoenixville, Pa.

REF: Letter of Appreciation

Dear Raymond:

Upon my departure from Valley Forge General Hospital I would like to thank you for your assistance in creating good liason between the 28th General Hospital and the Valley Forge General Hospital home unit. In a difficult intermediate position you have performed with sincerity a high regard for your men and a marked degree of finese. Without your efforts I feel that at times we would have been hopelessly bogged down.

I hope you continue to find success and happiness in all endeavors.

Yours sincerely,

Robert E. Lynch

ROBERT E. LYNCH, Major, MC
Chief of Radiology Service

SIGFM/SM 201.22 (19 May 58) 1st Ind
SUBJECT: Letter of Appreciation

HOSPITAL DETACHMENT (61-1301-1) Patterson Army Hospital, Fort Monmouth, New Jersey 20 May 1958

TO: SFC Raimondo Visciano RA 39 938 097 Hospital Detachment (61-1301-1) Patterson Army Hospital, Fort Monmouth, New Jersey

It is with great pleasure that I forward this letter and add my personal expression of appreciation.

Harry R. Zielazinski

HARRY R. ZIELAZINSKI
Major MSC
Commanding

PATTERSON ARMY HOSPITAL
Fort Monmouth, New Jersey

TO: Troop Commander, PAH
FROM: Chief, x-ray section, PAH   27 June 1958

    I would like to express my appreciation to Sfc. Raimondo Visciano for the co-operation which he gave me during my assignment at Patterson Army Hospital. He was NCOIC for the year prior to my arrival when a radiologist was not assigned to the hospital. He also was in charge during those trying months when the x-ray section numbered but two technicians and one on-the-job trainee.

    Sfc. Visciano is a skilled x-ray technician and an excellent non-commissioned officer. He has considerable ability in supply, administrative, and secretarial fields. The section has never had secretarial or administrative assistance, this job was acomplished by Sfc. Visciano in addition to his work as a technician.

    In a hospital such as this it was frequently necessary for me to absent myself from the department. For a period of time I was in the outpatient service each afternoon. Whenever I could not be present in the department I could be sure that every job would be properly performed under the supervision of Sfc. Visciano.

    Most important to me was the courteous and tactful manner in which Sfc. Visciano performed these many duties. In the constant turmoil engendered by too much work and too few technicians he was always kind and considerate to all patients. On many occasions this produced sincere expressions of gratitude from these patients.

    I would not hesitate to recommend Sfc. Visciano for any job of responsibility. I believe that his technical and administrative ability bring credit to the service.

Stephen M. Ayres, Capt MC
Chief, radiology section

Department of the Army

Certificate of Training

This is to certify that

SFC RAIMONDO VISCIANO, RA39938097

has successfully completed

TECHNIQUES OF WORK SIMPLIFICATION

Given at Fort Dix, New Jersey

21 July 1961

R. H. TUCKER
Maj Gen USA
Commanding

DA FORM 87, 1 SEP 54 REPLACES DA FORM 87, 1 JAN 49, WHICH IS OBSOLETE

VISCIANO, Raimondo   1st Ind
SUBJECT: Certificate of Achievement

Troop Command, 28th General Hospital, Phoenixville, Pennsylvania, 15 Apr 64

TO: SFC E6 Raimondo Visciano, RA 39 938 097 28th General Hospital, Phoenixville, Pennsylvania

I would like to commend you for the outstanding performance of duty that led to the commendatory remarks.

WILLIAM J. STANDIFER
Capt, MSC
Troop Commander

3 Incl
1. Ltr Transmittal
2. Ltr Achievement
3. Certificate

HEADQUARTERS
US ARMY HOSPITAL MUENCHWEILER (225TH STATION HOSPITAL)
APO 189, US Forces

AEUHM-M   19 March 1964

SUBJECT: Letter of Transmittal

TO: Commanding Officer
28th General Hospital
Valley Forge Pennsylvania

1. Attention is invited to the inclosed citation for Sfc Visciano, Raimondo, RA 39 938 097.

2. It is requested that the inclosed citation be presented to Sfc Visciano at an appropriate ceremony.

FOR THE COMMANDER:

SHIRLEY J LINDEN
1st Lt, MSC
Adjutant

I Incl
Citation

HEADQUARTERS
2ND GENERAL HOSPITAL
APO 180   US FORCES

CERTIFICATE OF ACHIEVEMENT

As NCOIC of the X-Ray Department, 225th Station Hospital, Muenchweiler, Germany, SFC Raimondo Visciano, RA 39938099, AMEDS, distinguished himself by outstanding and meritorious service during the period 6 August 1961 to 13 March 1964. SFC Visciano has performed his duties in a highly commendable manner by giving unselfishly of his time and experience to meet the needs of the 225th Station Hospital. SFC Visciano's willingness to improve the operation of the X-Ray Department has added greatly to the efficient accomplishment of this hospital's mission. His generous contribution of knowledge and skill acquired through his years of military experience have assisted in obtaining superior results in the X-Ray Department. His enthusiastic leadership gained him the respect and admiration of his superiors and subordinates. His mature and sound judgement in all phases of military life has been highly effective in counseling younger members of this organization. SFC Visciano by his demonstration of constant devotion to duty and loyalty to the United States Army Medical Service has brought great credit upon himself and the United States Army.

OFFICIAL:

JAMES D. COX
Major, MSC
Adjutant

DEPARTMENT OF THE ARMY
VALLEY FORGE GENERAL HOSPITAL
PHOENIXVILLE, PA. 19460

IN REPLY REFER TO

30 August 1966

LETTER OF APPRECIATION

SFC Raimondo Visciano

Dear Sgt. Visciano,

On your retirement from the service, I wish to extend to you my sincere thanks and appreciation for the excellent work you have performed since attached to the Radiology Service and serving as the non-commissioned officer in charge. In particular, your administrative assistance has been invaluable during the recent patient build-up and frequent relative shortage of personnel. During our association, your sincerity and conscientiousness has been a constant and excellent example for the younger technicians under your supervision.

As you leave the service, I wish you success and happiness in all future endeavors and hope that you will find them very satisfying. You leave with the knowledge that you will be missed by all.

If I can ever be of any assistance please do not hesitate to call upon me.

Sincerely yours,

HOWARD L. COPAS
Major, MC
Chief, Radiology Service

STATEMENT

Regarding: RAIMONDO VISCIANO, SFC, RA39938097, MOS 935.663

Since this individual reported to Valley Forge General Hospital approximately 8 months ago it was most apparent from the start that he was cooperative and able. There are no phases of technical radiology which he cannot do. This would include routine work as well as assist in special procedures such as bronchography and angiography. He has demonstrated that he is a leader by the manner he governs the members of the 28th General Hospital under him.

To officially verify his competence he is a member of: The American Registry of Radiologic Technologists and American Society of Radiologic Technologists.

He has repeatedly shown he has well directed ambition. He is presently attending an off post course in Algebra and has made personal inquiries into attending an extensive and expensive course in Radioactive Isotopes in Philadelphia.

He is quick to assume added responsibilities and is presently training another individual in the essentials of radiologic technology.

If problems arise in the dark room or file room this individual can be assigned there and will straighten them out.

He is not the type to stand idly by when things need be done. This man is a credit to himself, the Army and the Radiology Department at Valley Forge General Hospital.

ROBERT E. LYNCH, Major, MC
Chief, Radiology Service

...Published in Port St. Lucie,Fl., Raimondo Visciano - Editor

574 SW Belmont Circle,3495[illegible]
Telephone (*) 336-0866 Publisher: Comandante Carlo Fava
Distributed twice yearly: May and November - Vol 1/88 May Issue
News of interest to the one time inhabitants at Fort Missoula,Montana

Italian Seaman Internment Camp

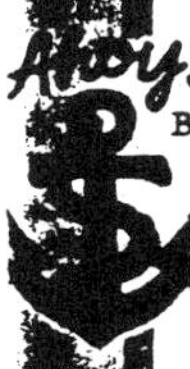
Ahoy!

Dateline: Port St. Lucie,Florida,-An "ad hoc committee of three had a reunion at the residence of Raimondo Visciano,ex Belvedere, after a separation of more than 45 years... Capt.Carlo Fava, ex Dino, now retired and living in Fort Lauderdale,Florida and Pietro Barresi,ex Conte Biancamano, also retired (what else at this stage?) living in Cincinnati,Ohio but vactioning in the Winter time in Pampano Beach,Florida,. were the other two Missoula "veterans". After a live session of rehashing memories, it was unanimously decided to create this form of communication in order to seek out as many as possible out of the 1,000 plus Fort Missoula tenants... Will you help?.. It is easy; all you have to do is to contact our enterpring editor, Raimondo Visciano and supply,names, news,and all the "gassip" you can assemble about other ex tenants.. in fact, the committee even proposed to create an identification of the category that would be factual,descreptive and, at same time carry a touch of "romanticism"...from the Mother land with an historical flavor... How about, if we were to identify ourselves as "the garibaldini of Fort Missoula"?... The "garibaldini" of the Rinascimento were about 1,000 as was the population of the Camp, approximately;their goal was to further the cause of Italy's unification to grow up to a respected, strong unit among the world's large nations;likewise,the new breed of Missoula (or Montana if you so profer) garibaldini,played an important role in the last world configration,contribuiting energies,talents,and dignity...gaining an eventful spot in the history of World War II. As we grew up, back home, we learned in school of their high patriotic value under their leader Giuseppe Garibaldi,and we also cultivate a deep respect for them,especially when,during any of the patriotic parade their presence grew thinner with passing of time. We do too grow thinnerin number...and this is the reason for creating this form of "reaching out to each other" and share dear memories and past emotions...that,added to our achievements in the years past Fort Missoula create a solid present... We have a lot to tell each other... we have a lot to share...so that our own families;our own siblings,too could find and appreciate hidden value born out of hardship and yes,out of unjustified captivity.. like all else in nature,these men were able to harvest the fruit of their labor, dedication and dignity in a land that turned from hostile at the beginning, into a golden opportunity offering all of us a chance to sprout and exploit...This is today,the image of the "Montana Garibaldino"yanked from the tradition of skill in seameship to land over the Rocky Mountains in the Far West... and then moving along the new discoveries,new adventures,new developments... family,children,..business and success in the effort. This is our initial presentation...There are no fees.. but,please join us..tell a friend, a lost "Montana Garibaldino" so that he too will share.....

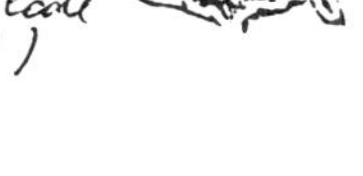
Missoula

After April 16, 1988 the new area code will be: (407)

A newslette

From: Mr. Raimondo Visciano

Here is a letter written in Italian, in answer to a request by one of our friends in Florida. They have tried to research the families, relatives or friends, but so far with no success.

Reading this short story would make you think of the confusion of the war. During the Second World War, many innocent people were lost without notice even by their families and relatives. Some people are forgotten regardless of their nationalities.

The three men who I am mentioning in this short story are: Dr. Giusepppe Marchese, Catania, Sicilia, Italy: 1918-1942. Aurelio Mariano, Genova Italy: 1914-1943. Giuseppe Marrazzo, Torre Del Greco, Napoli, Italy: 1896-1943.

These three men are buried in Missoula at Saint Mary Cemetery. They were Italian internees at Fort Missoula, Montana, who died while they were on the Campus. They were buried at the expense of the United States Department of Immigration. However, the Immigration Service apparently never sent a letter to their families. On the other hand, no one ever claimed the loss of these three people -- even the Italian government in Sicilia and Genova, and the United States. These three men were forgotten by their families and by the agencies of navigation to which they once belonged.

However, there is some human consciousness to be taken into consideration. Mr. and Mrs. Alfredo Cipolato, who operated for many years the Broadway Market in

Missoula. They knew the three Italians and, for the sake of their conscience, for fifty years or so went on All Saints Day to put flowers on their graves and considered the men as belonging to their family. Mr. Cipolato knew them when they were at Fort Missoula.

After many years the idea came to us to make a stone for their graves, at our expense. After all, they were innocent people who for some inexplicable reason died in Missoula.

Attached here is the Italian letter written by the Captain of the Coast Guard, telling us that they would do some research concerning their families, if some could be found. So far there have been no results. This story and many others like this one are taken for granted. On the contrary, it reflects the feelings of many Christians of all denominations that unless we are very famous, we are never mentioned by name again, but are just dumped together as "the deceased," someone else's ancestors.

Lord, grant them happiness in eternity. Alleluia.

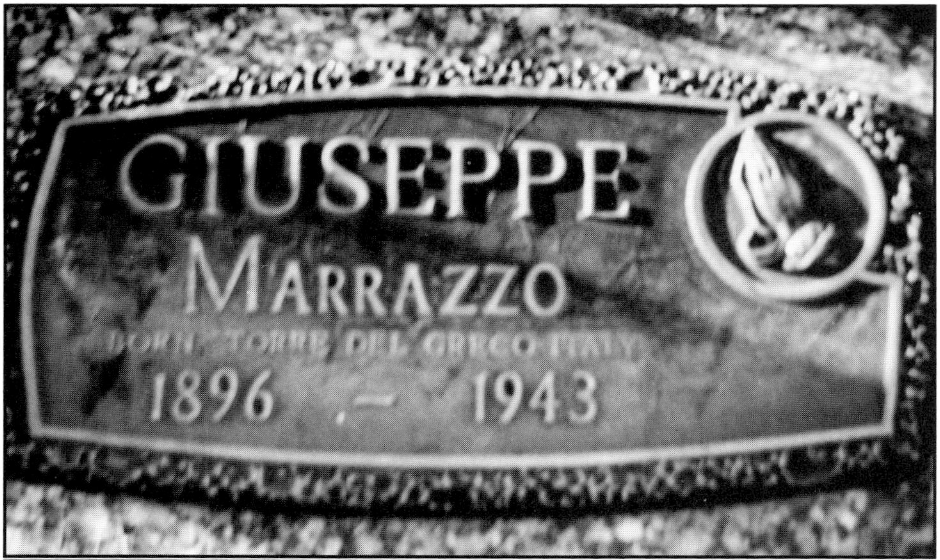
GIUSEPPE
MARRAZZO
BORN TORRE DEL GRECO ITALY
1896 – 1943

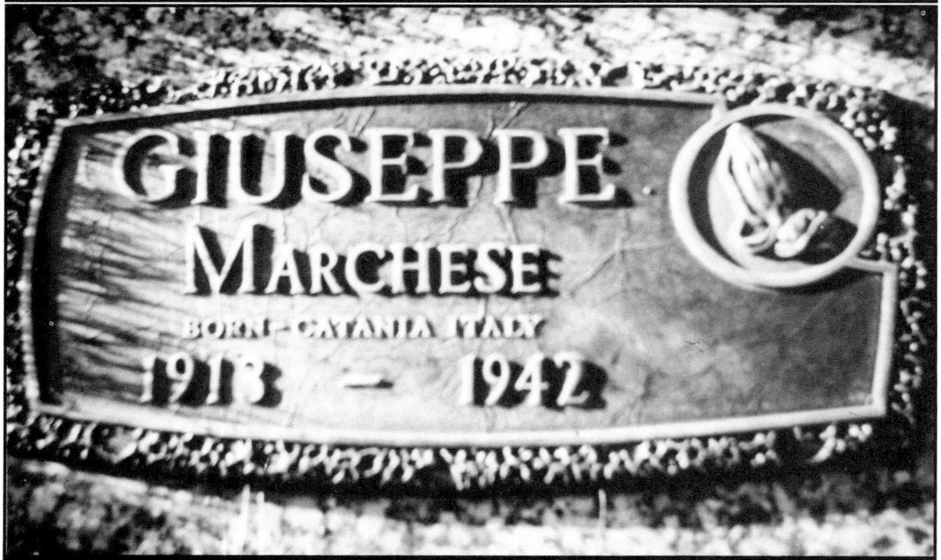
GIUSEPPE
MARCHESE
BORN CATANIA ITALY
1913 – 1942

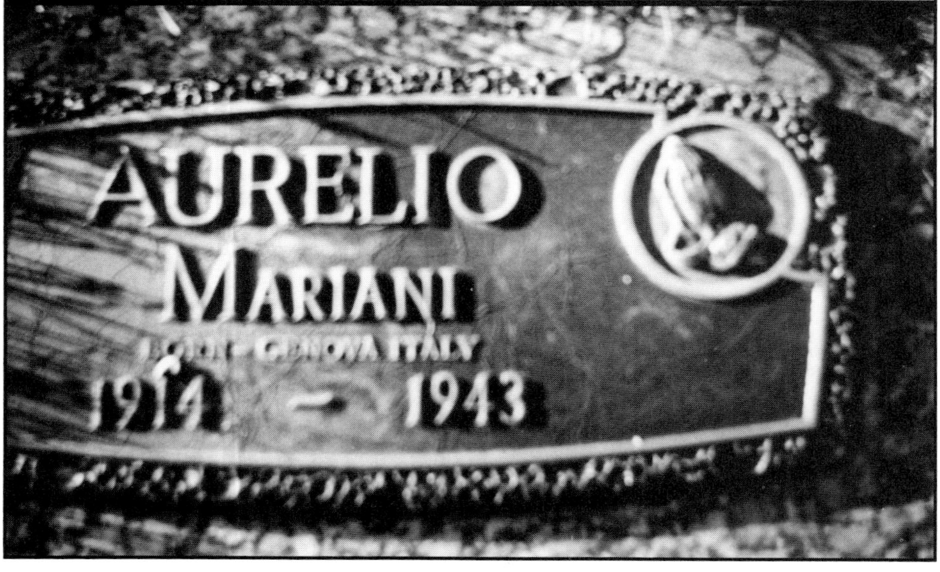
AURELIO
MARIANI
BORN GENOVA ITALY
1914 – 1943

Collegio Nazionale Patentati Capitani

Lungo Corso e Direttori Macchina

Ente Riconosciuto dal Min. Marina Mercantile con D. M. 9-1-1976

Delegazione di Catania

Catania, lì 19 Maggio 1988

DELEGATO: Dott. Cap. L. C. VLADIMIRO FUOCHI
SEDE SOCIALE: Via Aloi n. 47 - 95128 CATANIA
ABITAZIONE: Via G. De Felice n. 91 - 95128 CATANIA - Tel. (095) 32.76.16

Egr.
Sg. Raimondo VISCIANO
574 SW Belmont
PORT ST. LUCIE FL
34953 U.S.A.

Prot. n.
Vs. Rif.
Oggetto:

Gent.mo Sg. Raimondo Visciano,

per un disguido postale ricevo solo oggi la Sua gradita lettera del 20 Marzo 1988.

Le devo confessare che mentre la leggevo una grande commozione ha invaso il mio cuore ; è nobile ciò che Lei insie= me con i Sigg. Paolillo, Benedetti e Cipollato avete fatto per i nostri cari Colleghi deceduti lontani dal suolo Patrio.

Sarà mia premura e preciso compito svolgere le accu= rate indagini sia presso la Capitaneria di Porto di Catania sia presso il locale Comune.

Inoltre, Le sarei veramente grato se mi può comunica= re sia i nomi che gli indirizzi, che Lei conosce, dei nostri Colleghi Ufficiali e Marinai che vivono ancora nella sua città.

Sarebbe molto bello il poter organizzare un incontro qui a Catania di tutti i reduci del mare.

Rimango in attesa di una Sua gentile risposta e spero nella mia prossima lettera di darLe buone notizie.

A nome degli Equipaggi della Marina Italiana e mio personale La ringraziamo e porgo cordiali saluti.

Collegio Nazionale Patentati Capitani L. C. e D. M. - CATANIA

Cap.L.C. Dott. Vladimiro FUOCHI

Vladimiro Fuochi

[handwritten at top: Per [Umberto] - Courtesy of John Alfredo Cipolato — Grazie! C.F.]

CAPTAIN CARLO FAVA
2137 Northeast 63 Court
Fort Lauderdale, Florida 33308

May 2, 1989

Dear Umberto:

It is again my pleasure to extend congratulations for your accomplishments. I am grateful to the Cipolato's for sending to me a tear sheet from the "Bitter Root Senior Citizen" ' Spring Edition with the interesting article by Mark Ratledge. Knowing how modest you are I would not have had the privilege of reading it.

A very touching, humane story...unique in its account, and yet entirely understandable and appreciable. I assume, the house is still standing there as a monument to the gracefulness and charm of her perennial fleeting image...Katherine, was her name that, from what I conjure, is indelebly written in your mind. A lovely story, indeed.

I am taking the liberty of sending the tear sheet to our colleague Raimondo Visciano - 574 SW Belmont Circle, Port St. Lucie, Florida 34953 - who is the efficient coordinator for all our colleagues interned at Fort Missoula during World War II. He is very accurate and much up to-date; should you ever need information about that period and afterwards, please do not hesitate to contact him: he is most accommodating. And, while on this subject I must regretfully announce the demise of Peter Barresi - ex Conte Biancamano - who passed away a month ago here in Fort Lauderdale where he usually spent the Winter months with his lovely wife Molly. I got to know him quite well and I miss him very much; both of them became very close to us and together we shared some pleasant times every Winter... "I ranghi si assottigliano sempre piu'".. caro Umberto, nell'ordine naturale della vita stessa.

Stay well; keep in touch and carry on with the same enthusiasm all your academic projects; in time, I shall appreciate reading more of your works, especially with curiosity about your study and research on "life". All the best, ever.

Sincerely,

Carlo Fava

Mr. Umberto Benedetti
c/o M/M A. Cipolato
602 E. Broadway
Missoula, Montana 59802

cc: R. Visciano

P.S. - Reportedly,"Che Bella Vista" were the words of young man Peter Barresi upon arriving at Fort Missoula after a 4-day barred train tiresome ride from New York's Ellis Island to the new residence... *in 1941*

Capt. Paolo Stefano Saglietto
The Second Mayor of the Fort

Capt. Paolo Stefano Saglietto, the second Mayor of the Fort. De Luca Alessandro, 1st Captain Commissariat, was the first Mayor of the Fort in 1941. De Luca and Capt. Francesco La Rosa, 2nd Officer, both from the *Il Conte Biancamano*, were the first ones to come to the Fort with some officers of the Immigration and Naturalization Services to assess the location and climate of the site. They wanted to see if the sailors coming from warmer climates could adjust to the cold Montana temperatures.

John Battista Paolillo
Another True Story of a Fort Missoula Boy

John Paolillo, from Torre del Greco (Naples), Italy, began working aboard the *SS Guidonia*, a private shipping liner. After about a half dozen voyages between Italy, Northern Europe, and Thailand, his ship sailed into U.S. waters. Arriving in Newport News, Virginia, the plan was to load coal and return to Genova, Italy. But in the year 1939, turbulent times led to political intrigue. The coal was never loaded and the *SS Guidonia* was prevented from sailing. The ship was in the harbor for eight months, and in 1940, armed members of the U.S. Coast Guard went on board and confiscated the ship, together with about 28 Italian vessels all over the United States that were docked or anchored in U.S. ports at the time.

The crews, totalling about 1,200 sailors, were taken to an internment camp at Fort Missoula, Montana. They were transported on trains with bars on the windows as "civilian internees." After spending about three years at Fort Missoula, the authorities decided to put these internees to work.

John Paolillo was chosen to work for the Sisters of Charity at Saint Thomas, an orphanage located in Great Falls, Montana. At the time, they were "John Guardian Angels." Paolillo was the only civilian internee who worked there (from 1942-1944), doing carpentry and as a boiler room engineer. He learned to speak English gradually and by necessity.

Although he still has no idea how it happened, John received a notice saying that he was drafted into the U.S. Army Infantry in 1944. After receiving basic training in California and spending some time there, he was sent to Camp Kilmer in New Jersey. A week later, he was shipped overseas to France to attend Military Police School.

Upon his graduation, he was assigned to Frankfurt-Main in Germany. After almost two years of duty with the Military Police 709 Service Battalion Headquarters Command, he accepted a discharge in order to work with the European Exchange System as a Security Supervisor.

John came back to Missoula, Montana, to see again the fort at which he was interned, and then went to Great Falls to see his benefactors at the Sisters of Charity and at the Saint Thomas orphanage. However, after so many years most of the sisters were retired. Nonetheless, he went to Spokane, Washington, to see the Sisters of Charity who had retired there and whom he had loved. It was a very happy reunion.

In conclusion, John Paolillo fulfilled his dreams by returning to Montana to see his friends. Sadly, it was later found that he had cancer, and he passed away on Feb. 2, 1990.

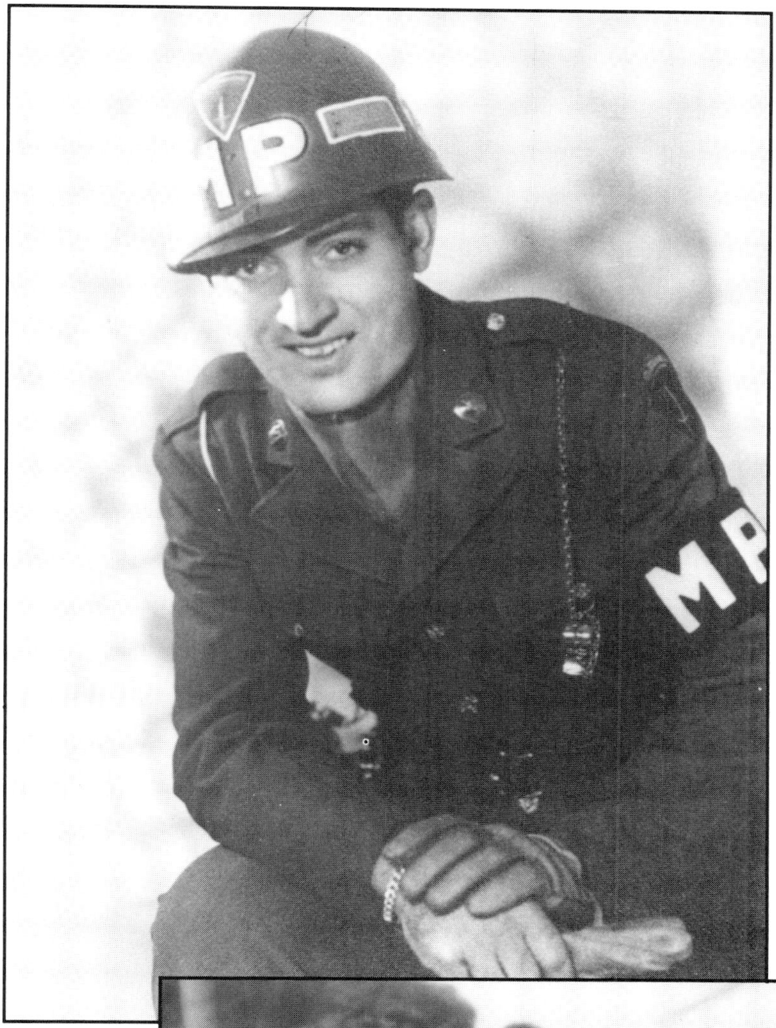
MP
MP

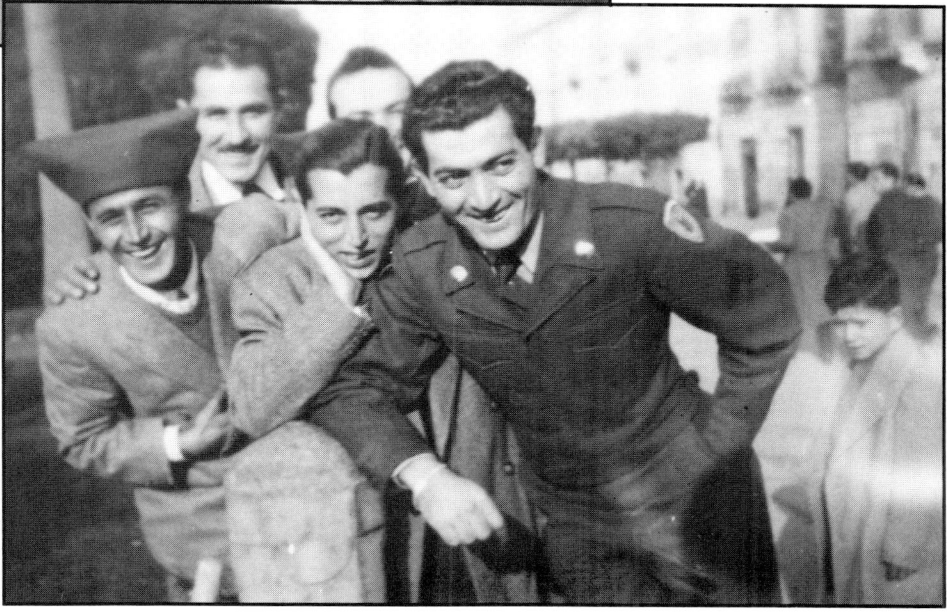

This is Agostino Ronzitti from Genova, Italy. I know a little story about this soldier. An only child with a good social status, he was working at the New York World's Fair during 1939-1940 and was interned at Fort Missoula with other World's Fair personnel. After he was released from the Fort, he spent three years in the American Army serving in England. He risked his life without saying anything to his parents. After the war ended, he married an Austrian woman and opened a restaurant back East. He is still living there. Destiny plays an important role in our lives—he left Genova and became an American.

War Restrictions on Enemy Aliens

■ There is a need for clarification. In the interest of historic accuracy I must address the assertion that no Germans or Italians were affected by the government's relocation ("Japanese-Americans Mourn an Old Friend," Jan. 8).

While it was determined after much debate that Executive Order 9066 would be restricted in its application to Japanese aliens and citizens, other enemy alien groups were also affected by World War II. On Dec. 7, 1941, the Enemy Alien Control Unit of the Justice Department, citing Section 21, Title 50 of the U.S. Code and Presidential Proclamation 2525, apprehended 1,000 enemy aliens, 48 in the Los Angeles area.

On Dec. 16, 1941, detainees at Terminal Island including 110 Germans, 364 Japanese and 25 Italians were transferred under FBI supervision to internment facilities at Ft. Missoula and Ft. Lincoln, Mont. By June, 1942, 8,500 enemy aliens had been incarcerated. An additional 2,364 citizens from Axis countries residing in Latin America were interned in INS camps in Texas.

It should be noted that at the same time similar sweeps were occurring in Canada.

Enemy aliens not in custodial detention were required to register and were subjected to numerous restrictions.

Beginning in January, 1942, local authorities and FBI agents using executive search warrants issued by the Justice Department searched enemy alien homes for contraband including photographic equipment and flashlights. In addition, on March 24, 1942, a curfew was imposed on all Southern California enemy aliens, confining them to their homes between 8 p.m. and 6 a.m., and restricting non-work-related travel to a five-mile radius.

The wartime emergency also called for the evacuation of enemy aliens from strategic locations. On Feb. 1, 1942, the Los Angeles Times reported that Germans, Italians and Japanese would be removed from 69 zones including Downey, Vernon and parts of Santa Monica, adding that "the aged and the infirm will not be allowed to remain with naturalized sons and daughters in such areas." Though placards bearing evacuation instructions in German, Japanese and Italian were posted, comprehensive relocation was carried out only at Terminal Island and along the Northern California coast.

The sheer numbers of potential internees and political expediency ultimately confined the thrust of Executive Order 9066 to Japanese aliens and citizens. But the burden of restrictions, regulation and, to some extent, detention was also borne by German and Italian aliens.

GLORIA RICCI LOTHROP
Professor of History
Cal Poly Pomona

Donato Giuseppe Incoronato

Donato Giuseppe Incoronato was born on Jan. 27, 1921, in Resina, a suburb of Naples, Italy. He grew up in Civitavecchia, the Port of Roma, Italy. His family settled in Naples about 250 years ago and were commercial fishermen. Donato's father broke that tradition when he became a seaman. During the Greco-Roman War, Resina was called Herculaneum, but after World War II the name was changed to Ercolano, as it is known today. The town is near Torre del Greco. There are small towns close to each other, with coastline beaches. Archaeologists still dig there, the Historical Roman Artifacts. Incoronato was with the boat "Dino" in Boston Harbor when World War II began in the United States. The U.S. Immigration Service picked up all the crew and sent them to Fort Missoula, Montana, in 1941.

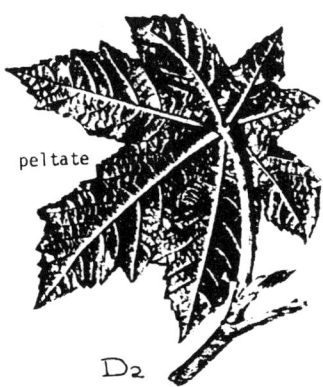

Photos from Carole Incoronato Toppins Collection

Donato Giuseppe Incoronato was one of 1,200 internees at Fort Missoula. He started to work for the Great Northern Railroad. The wages were low, the benefits few, and the hours were long. Track crews often worked six days a week for 10 or more hours a day and were often called out on their day off or in the middle of the night for train derailments.

Donato became involved with the Employees Union. He held every position at one time or another, including serving as union president. He was a grievance officer for 12 years and quietly fought for workers' rights. With the help of others, they succeeded in gaining improvements peacefully.

Donato had a cheerful, outgoing personality. He enjoyed being with people and had a lot of friends. He kept in touch with the Italian internees in Helena and Butte and those in Philadelphia. But his friends came from all walks of life.

His family always came first. Donato refused any job that would require him to travel while his children were growing up. He died on April 16, 1983.

His wife, Jean, (pictured below on right) was born on January 27, 1919, and grew up in Everett, Washington. She was in the Navy Hospital Corps in Helena, Montana, and later worked for the State Government Employment Office.

A true love story:

Age and circumstances do not exist for love. Donato Incoronato met and fell in love with Jean Elizabeth Cole, and they married. Both wife and husband contributed their labors for humanitarian purposes in American society. The following pictures are of Jean in different places.

These were part of 28 ships that were in eastern harbors when the United States interned them in 1941. The crews were eventually sent to internment at Fort Missoula.

When one boat was taken, the crew was playing a card game on deck. Donato Incoronato was on the *S/S Dino* in Boston Harbor. Captain Fava was in command. The captain remained in the United States after the war living in Boston and passed away a few years ago in Florida.

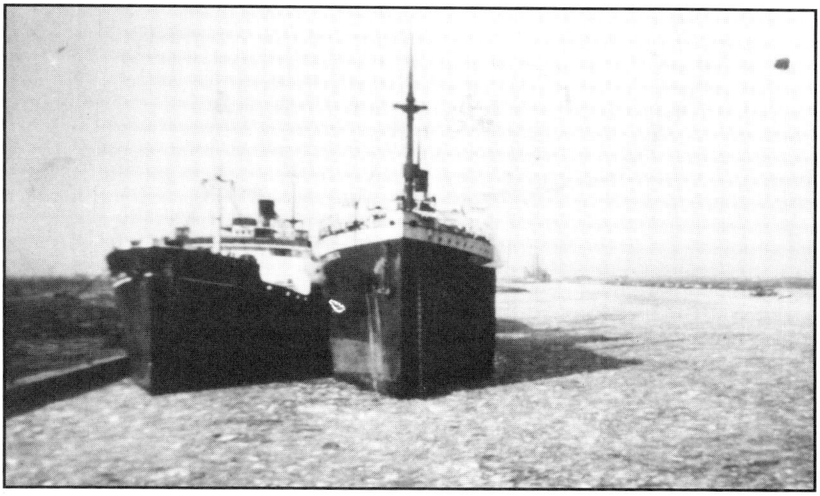

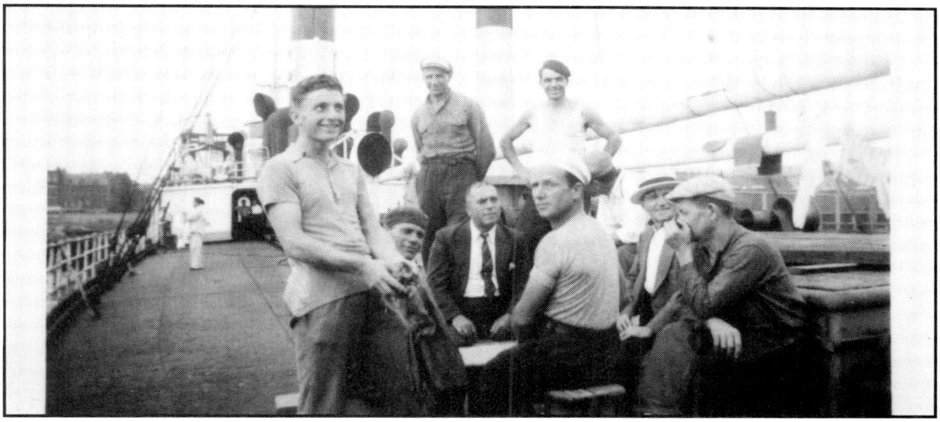

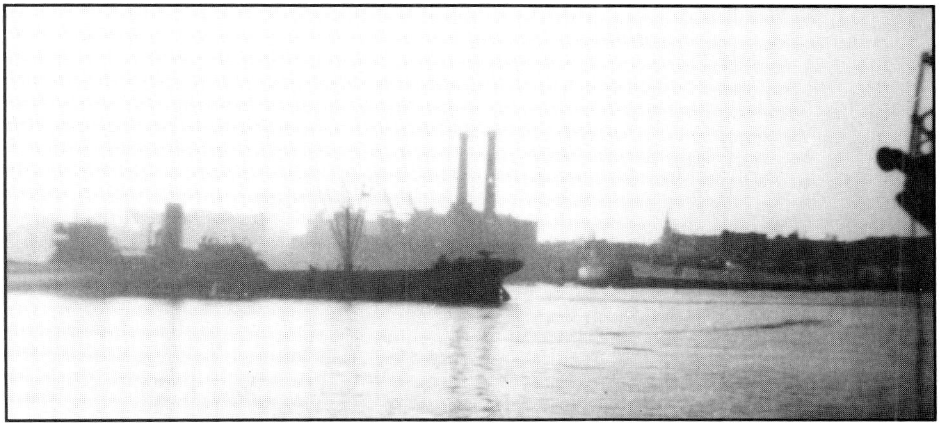

This American frigate, anchored in Boston Harbor, was watching the ships and activities of the crews. The practice by U.S. Navy ships was common whether the foreign ships were Italian, German or Japanese.

A Northern Pacific train arrives in Missoula with detainees to be interned at Fort Missoula.

This is Fort Missoula in 1941-1943. Here began the true friendship of neighbors without fear. The lady arrives with a bucket of cool water for workers. We were all treated as part of the Missoula community.

Fort Missoula was a melting pot for all types of sailors. Regardless of social status or crew position, whether deck boy or captain, they had become good friends during the internment years, and spoke with each other despite regional language differences.

Sunday festivities after the 9:00 a.m. Mass. The brass band performed all kinds of songs for their comrades. This broke the monotony of camp life and alleviated some of their family worries.

The internees are enjoying a Sunday afternoon soccer game.

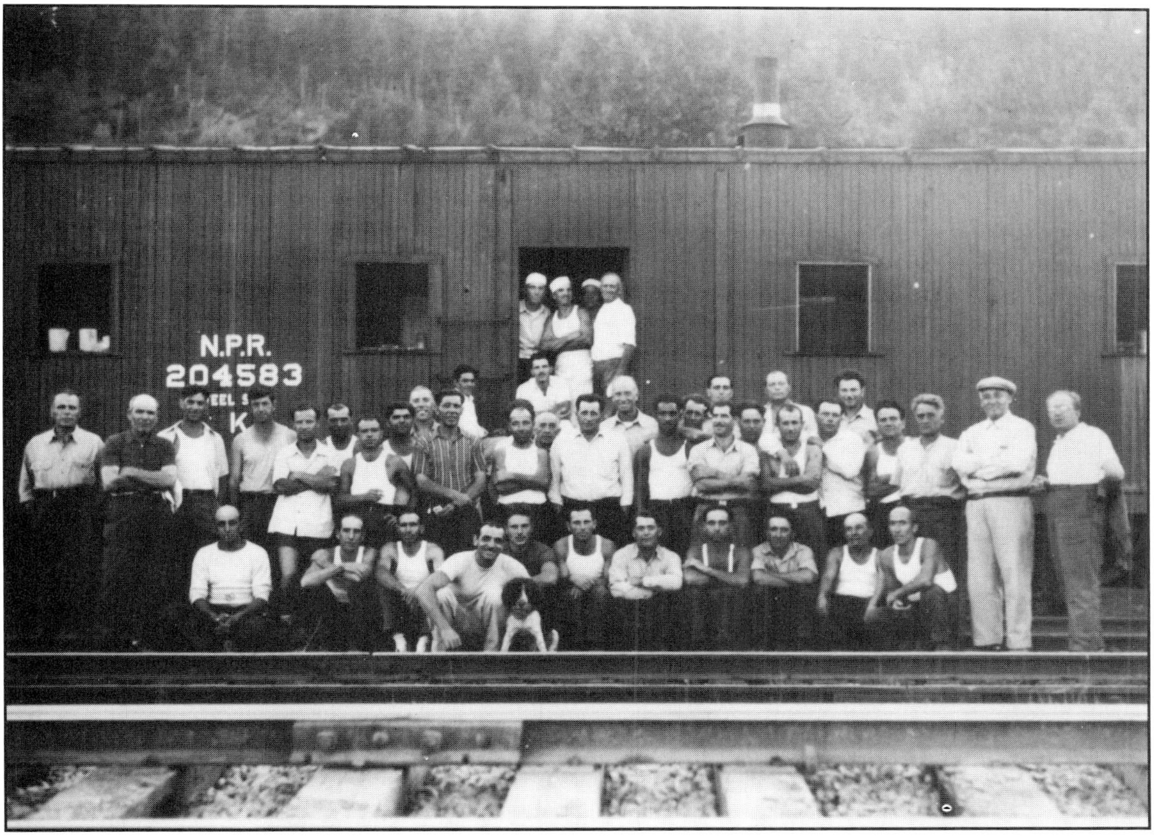
N.P.R.
204583

The Power of Labor Man

Labor is the prime basic
condition for all human
existence. In a sense, we
have to say that labor
created man himself.
Umberto Benedetti

During World War II the United States suffered a severe labor shortage due to millions of men in uniform. Internees, such as these men from Fort Missoula, were put to work on the farms and transportation systems. The Fort Missoula internees first organized themselves within the camp and then were hired for outside labor. They were never recognized for their contributions to the War effort.

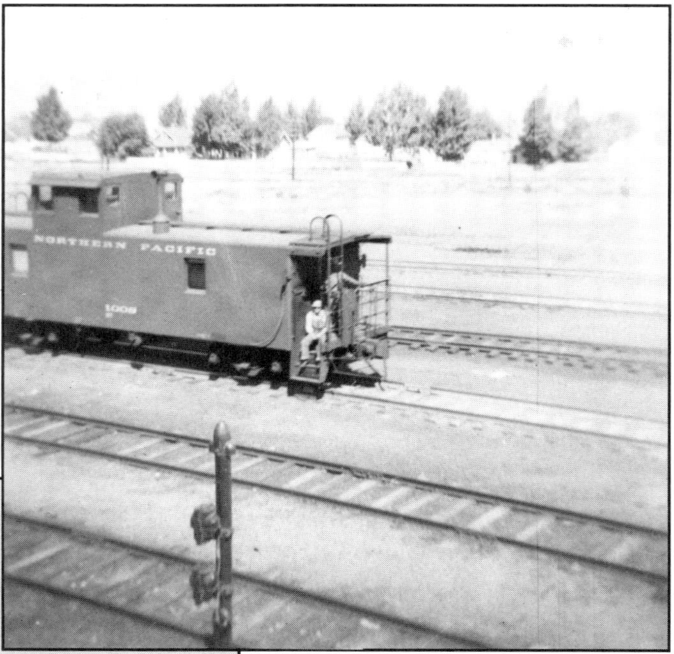
NORTHERN PACIFIC
1008

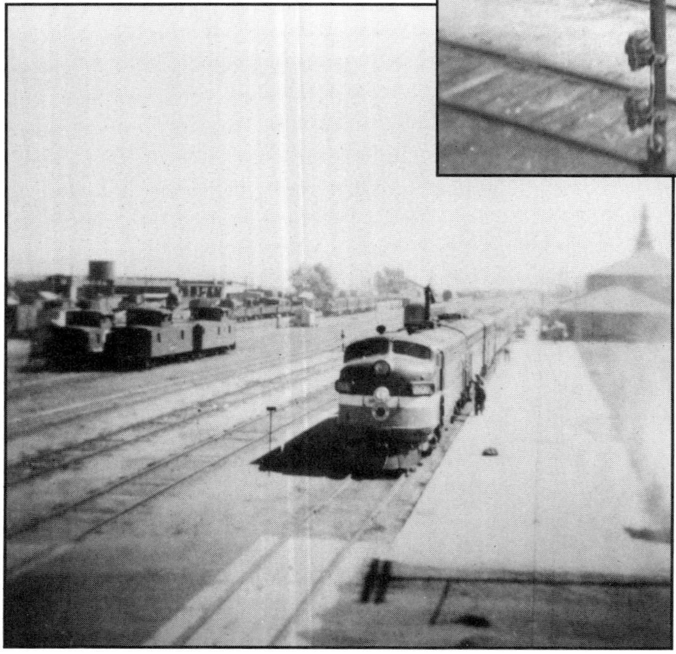

From sailors to railroad men. Without even knowing the English language these men had pride in their work. Some of these workers went unrecognized to their eternal repose. Alleluia.

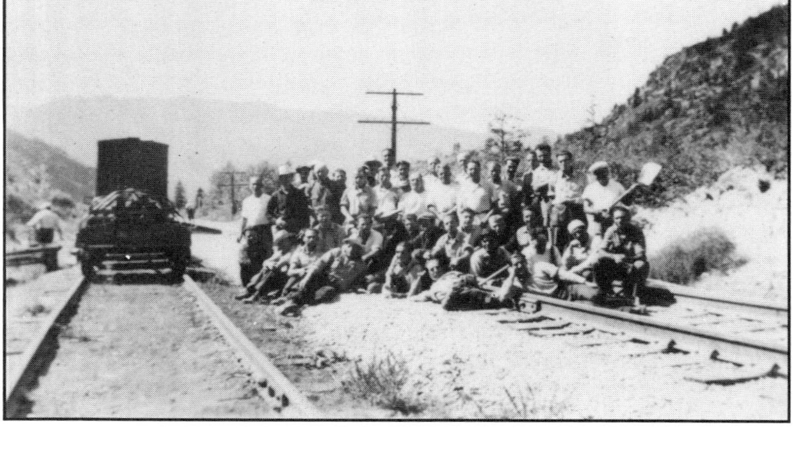

Italians working on the Northern Pacific Railroad.

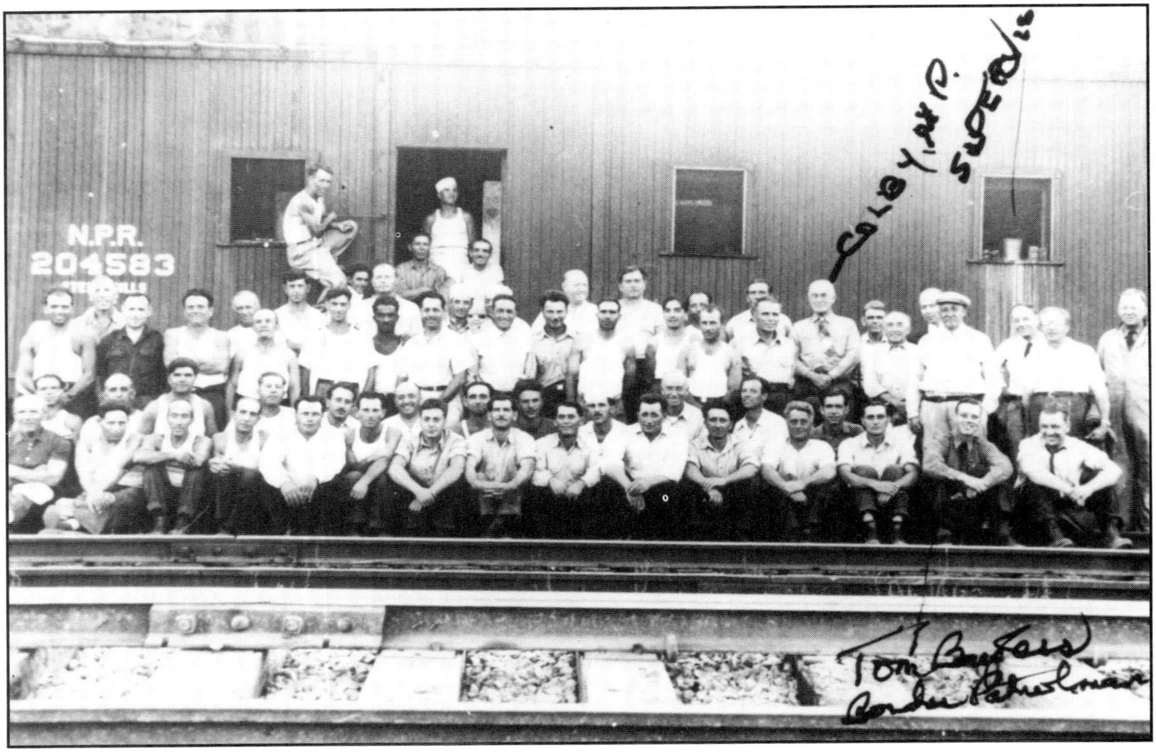
N.P.R.
204583

This is the last crew that worked for the Northern Pacific Railroad. There are two signatures of their supervisors.

Vincent Rivieccio Collection

"History Cannot Be Written Without Facts"

Here is one of the facts that made history during World War II, when the boats were detained in the waters of the United States. The ship in the picture, *Il Leme* was anchored in Portland.

One of Seized Ships Here

Leme, 27 Other Italians Taken

(See Story on Page 1 Also)

The 6059-ton Italian motorship Leme, war-bound in the Columbia and Willamette rivers since June 7, 27 other Italian, at least 35 Danish and two German vessels in American ports were in custody of the United States coast guard Sunday—their future activities undetermined.

While Captain Giovanni Polonio, Chief Officer John Polli, Stewardess Louisa Steinbach and other officers and members of the crew were quartered in the immigration detention rooms at the county courthouse, armed coast guardsmen patroled the Leme and allowed no civilians aboard.

Hammers Do Work

Ordered by Washington to seize the Leme to prevent damage and destruction, Lieutenant-Commander M. P. Jensen of the Astoria guard base and his men were too late when they boarded the ship early Sunday at her berth—the Northwestern grain dock south of Swan Island airport.

Every instrument of navigation had been put out of commission by hammer blows. All electric motors and generators were smashed.

Preliminary examination indicated that the crew had been operating the Leme's engines for the last two or three nights, by use of air compressors, and that emery dust had been placed in the lubricating oil in an endeavor to wreck or destroy the motors.

Crew Not Dejected

Every instrument on the bridge except the gyro or stabilizer had been demolished.

Below decks, corresponding instruments in the engine room had been battered with hammers, control levers were battered or broken, the outside casings of electric motors had been smashed and ripped to fragments and the interior mechanism destroyed.

The engine room was oil-splashed and littered.

The singing, wine-drinking crew assembled on the deck appeared far from dejected about the damage to the 500-foot motorship or their detention.

Leme Built in 1925

Members of the crew ranged in age from a youthful wiper of about 19 to grizzled old-time men.

For the last two or three months members of the crew had been studying the English language under the tutelage of a WPA instructor, sent to the vessel once a week by request after a few members had attended a regular language class ashore.

The Leme, largest vessel in the Italian Line service on the Pacific coast, was built at Trieste in 1925.

She sailed out of the Columbia river June 7 but immediately received orders from the Italian government to return, and re-entered the Columbia June 8. In September the Leme was brought to Portland.

Seizure of the Leme was complicated by a libel and attachment brought against the Italian line and the vessel last June by Cia Bananera Nacional and Alejos & Cia, two Guatemalan concerns, in an effort to collect $137,000 for fuel oil.

Warships on Watch

The coast guard has been under instructions since June 11 to prevent the Leme from leaving the Columbia river pending settlement of the action.

Another reason for the Leme's long idleness, however, was the vigilance of Canadian warships awaiting to capture the vessel should it reach the open Pacific.

Skipper of Italian Vessel Boarded in Portland Harbor Declares Maneuver Constitutes 'An Act of War'

BY RICHARD NOKES
Staff Writer, The Oregonian

The United States government Sunday committed "an act of war" against Italy when the coast guard seized the motorship Leme and incarcerated the Italian crew in the Multnomah county jail. Captain Giovanni Polonio, ship's commander since 1928, declared as he watched his men being hustled from the Northwest grain docks in patrol wagons. One sailor said, "war will be likely to come" as a result of the action.

Captain Polonio a moment later confirmed his belief in the seriousness of the coast guard move when, in response to the specific question "Do you believe this is an act of war?" he snorted "Of course!"

Act Called "Inhuman"

The handsome Italian sea captain sadly avowed; "I never expected to have an experience like this i.. this country. It is really inhuman what they are doing really improper."

When asked if He meant that it was improper according to international law, Captain Polonio replied, "I do not know. According to my judgment, yes. I have seen the last war, I am expressing that this is inhuman. Even prisoners of war we do not treat like this in Italy."

"This is inhuman," he shouted.

The mariner admitted with almost a smile that he and his crew had damaged the Leme. When asked, exactly what had been done, he answered, "We immobilized it. She can no longer move."

Asked the reason for taking such an action, Captain Polonio asserted, "She was going to be seized by your country—don't you understand this?"

Skipper Shrugs to Query

Later, asked who had given the order to sabotage the vessel, the captain merely shrugged. (A member of the crew said a "higher up" had given the order to the captain and to all other Italian ships in America.)

The Leme commander shook his head as though bewildered and complained, "We have respect for your law. Why do they take us to jail? We immobilized the ship but it is our ship. We do not set afire the docks, we do not sink the ship, we do no hurt to American property."

Captain Polonio expressed great concern over the jailing of his men. "None of them has been in jail before. They feel they haven't committed any crimes and jail is not the place for us."

He complained that none of them had time finished to shave nor eat breakfast before the coast guard took armed possession of the Leme at 7 A. M. "I was just getting up," he said.

WPA Classes Held

As the sailors chattered in more or less good English, the reporter expressed amazement that all apparently could speak the language of this country. Captain Polonio proudly declared that "every one speaks English. Your government (the WPA) has held classes for us on the ship twice a week for the last four months. All of the men go sometimes, meet at them go all the time."

One of the sailors requested that copies of The Oregonian be sent to them in jail because "we can all read English. We want to see what you say about us."

Nineteen-year-old Andrew Tonen said he had not heard from his family for three months and wanted to know if the letters had been censored by the American government.

Then he asked, "Is this not the United States where there is liberty and everything? You are no in war, you are in peace. Yours is the land of liberty. You can speak here. Why do you put us in jail?"

Tonen expressed gratification for the way the people of Portland had treated the Leme crew since last September. "Many people have been kind," he said.

Michael Gueidno, wireless operator, vociferously stated, "We have respect for law. We do not want to escape or nothing. Nobody has been in jail before. I am depressed."

All members of the crew, including Salvatore (I like to be called Sam) Garguilo, 17-year-old mess boy, had high praise for the American people. "We have had perfect freedom before, we have no complaints," was the way one grizzled veteran of the sea expressed it.

Captain Polonio denied that any of his men was intoxicated when the coast guard swooped. "When the coast guard came, we had had no breakfast," he said, "so we drank some of our champagne and other fine wines and ate salami."

The commander, sporting a tiny Italian emblem in his buttonhole, said that two of his crew were in the hospital. One, he said, had been operated on twice recently for eye trouble. Another, he said, "has diphtheria."

John Matthews, chief jailer, worried as to the type of treatment the seamen would get, said, "A little better than ordinary." He later said their first meal consisted of roast beef, mashed potatoes, gravy, four slices of bread, pears and coffee.

The 50 seamen were first herded into one large cell block which was serviced by only two toilets. The officers later were transferred to private quarters, Matthews said. He added that it cell block was overcrowded and some of the sailors would be moved to another block.

Big Italian Motorship At Portland Battered Before Crew Interned

(See Wirephoto Page, Also)

The United States coast guard Sunday took armed possession of the big Italian motorship Leme in Portland harbor and found her engines and navigation instruments damaged beyond repair. In other sections of the country similar guards were placed on 27 additional Italian, at least 35 Danish and two German ships. Guardsmen and police interned 54 officers and crew of the Leme in the Multnomah county jail while the customs service was inspecting the damage.

While the WPA had been conducting classes in English for the crew, the portbound Italians had been systematically wrecking the navigating facilities of the vessel, it appeared.

Job Quickly Done

The wrecking job was completed, it was learned, through the veil of official silence, within the last three days.

When Lieutenant-Commander M. P. Jensen of the Astoria coast guard base at Tongue point and a dozen of his men boarded the Leme, with harbor and city police, early Sunday they found the crew with their sea bags packed and ready.

The crew, assembled on deck, was drinking wine and singing Italian songs to the accompaniment of a guitar. One load of 12 seamen in a police patrol wagon sang lustily and happily en route through the city to the county jail.

Two in Hospital

Two of the Leme's crew are in a local hospital. One of those detained is a woman, Stewardess Louisa Steinbach. In jail also is the Leme's mascot, a friendly spaniel-terrier mutt.

Captain Giovanni Polonio, who hails from Trieste, was in excellent spirits. He grinned broadly when asked how badly the ship had been damaged, but replied in good English, "I don't know much about it."

Captain's Remark Overheard

Earlier he had been overheard in a declaration that "If the government of the United States is going to take over this ship it will be money ahead to install all new engines."

Commander Jensen refused to make a statement about the condition of the vessel and allowed no civilians aboard.

He said the coast guard had taken possession of the Leme on orders from Washington based on the necessity of "protecting navigation." He referred to a possibility that the crew might scuttle the vessel in the harbor. One estimate of the damage to the vessel was $185,000.

Roy J. Norene, immigration chief, received orders Sunday afternoon from department headquarters in Washington, D. C., officially placing the officers and crew, as aliens, in his custody.

More news of Leme on page 6.

The Oregonian

VOL. LXXX—NO. 25,082   PORTLAND, OREGON, MONDAY, MARCH 31, 1941   CITY EDITION

Scores of Axis and Danish Steamships Seized by U. S.; Leme, Here, Sabotaged

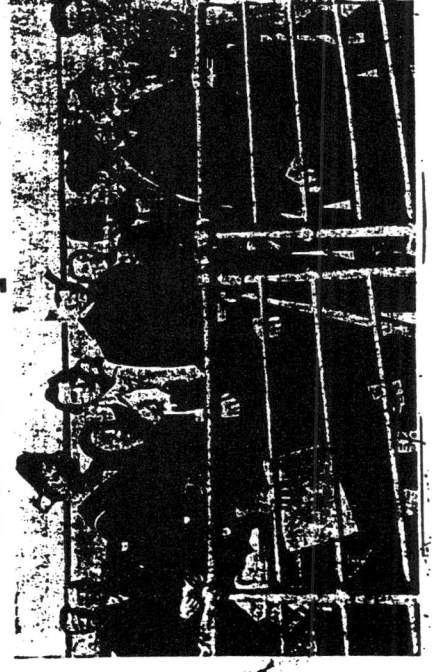

Crew Makes Total Wreck Of Italian Ship Machinery

BY LAWRENCE BARBER

(Editor's note: further text illegible)

By looking at this photo, one can see that many people who were innocent bystanders doing their jobs when the war broke out suffered. But after many years one can reflect on the conditions of that period of time and can read the true story. During the war, the reporters had to say that America was always right. If I had been an American reporter, I would have done the same thing to influence the readers.

THE OREGONIAN, THURSDAY, APRIL 3, 1941

Italian Ship Seized in Cuba Placed Under Guard

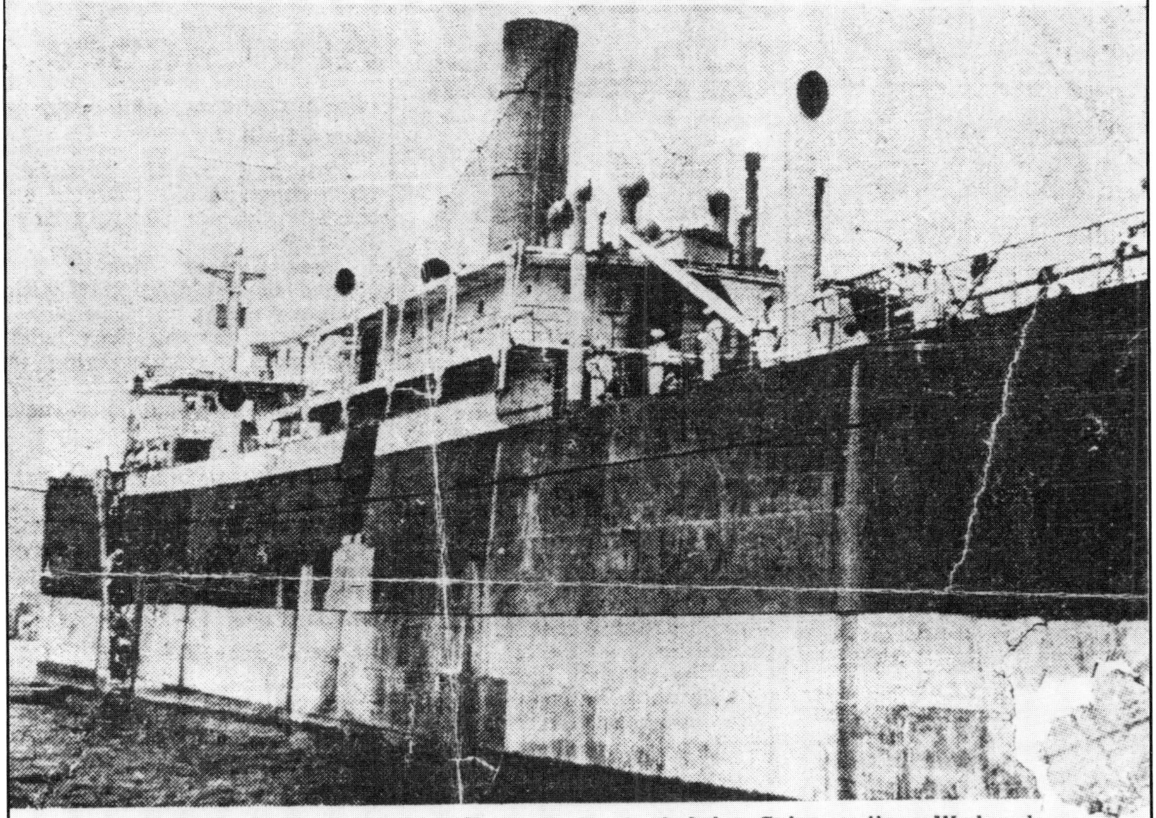

HAVANA The Italian freighter Recca was guarded by Cuban sailors Wednesd
Cuba seized Italian ships, following the United States' example. (AP W

This Italian freighter, *Recca*, was seized by Cuba, who was following America's policy. On the following pages can be read the story of private cargo boats along the coast during World War II.

Avevamo pubblicato lo scorso numero la cronaca della cerimonia rievocativa tenuta a Palazzo San Giorgio il 25 ottobre 1986 con la consegna delle pergamene ad alcuni protagonisti dell'episodio.

Abbiamo ritenuto di dedicare spazio al racconto avvincente e frutto di ricerche e documentazioni che ha scritto l'Ing. Francesco Scotto perché rimanga come testimonianza del valore della nostra gente di mare.

Dell'Ing. FRANCESCO SCOTTO

Sull'ultima guerra mondiale ed in particolare sulle sventurate vicende della nostra marina mercantile sono stati scritti fiumi di inchiostro, ma ritengo che non sia ancora di pubblico dominio l'episodio che vi voglio raccontare e che adesso vi sintetizzo in due parole:

«La sera del 10 Giugno '40, giorno dell'ingresso dell'Italia nella seconda guerra mondiale, 28 navi italiane giacevano all'ancora nei porti degli Stati Uniti d'America; dopo 10 mesi, il 29 Marzo del 1941 esse vennero improvvisamente e simultaneamente danneggiate dai loro equipaggi: perchè?».

Noi sappiamo quante tragedie abbia passato la nostra Marina ma soprattutto quante dimenticanze e talvolta quanto fango sia stato gettato su di essa e questo episodio è in linea invece con le nostre migliori tradizioni marinare.

Giudicherete voi quello che sentirete raccontare da me, che non sono nè uno storico nè un politico; questo ricordo di un episodio del '41 giudichiamolo nella giusta luce a 45 anni di distanza.

Io l'ho ricevuto dalla viva voce di uno dei protagonisti.

Passo a voi questo racconto, sicuro della sua autenticità comprovata da giornali, libri della Marina Militare e documenti dell'epoca che ho ricercato e sono qui a vostra disposizione; comprovato soprattutto qui dalla presenza di tanti ufficiali che il Collegio Capitani con tanto amore ha ricercato e che sono stati testimoni oculari — ma che dico — attori comprimari di pieno diritto di questi fatti.

Passiamo alla storia: come ho già detto, all'imbrunire del 10 Giugno 1940, giorno dello scoppio delle ostilità 28 navi italiane per circa 200.000 tonnellate di stazza pari al 5 per cento di tutta la flotta di allora, giacevano all'ancora nei porti U.S.A.

Si trattava di 27 navi da carico secco o petroliere più la Tn. «Pax Biancamano» che si trovava a Panama.

Ricordiamo che erano rimaste all'estero 212 navi per oltre 1.200.000 tonn. di S.L. pari al 35% della flotta mercantile e per di più la fetta più importante di detta flotta perchè composta tutta di navi oceaniche.

Il tutto a causa sia della fretta di Mussolini nel dichiarare la guerra sia a causa della necessità di tenere celata la notizia della dichiarazione di guerra il più possibile: magra consolazione era il fatto che la Germania il 2 Settembre del '39 non si era comportata diversamente ed aveva perso quasi la metà della sua flotta all'estero.

Nel libro di Dino Grandi, uscito recentemente, «Il mio Paese» è scritto che il ministro delle Comunicazioni Host Venturi apprese trasecolato della dichiarazione di guerra ascoltando il discorso che Mussolini faceva da Piazza Venezia a Roma.

Faccio una piccola parentesi. Quanto sopra appare invero strano perchè le 28 navi italiane soprammenzionate erano state raggiunte cinque giorni prima della dichiarazione di [...] bile.

Il morale degli equipaggi, dopo lo sbarco delle merci e qualche mese di disarmo in attesa di ordini era basso perchè i mass-media americani erano — ovviamente — non benevoli verso l'Italia di Mussolini ed i poveri marittimi, ovviamente soli, dimenticati e ignari di tutto, si sentivano coinvolti ingiustamente in questa campagna di stampa.

Solo alcuni italiani della colonia di New York avevano capito: i giornali alimentavano una certa campagna di stampa e si faceva un gran polverone parlando di quinta colonna, di spie: insomma Roosevelt con molta abilità tesseva la sua tela e preparava il paese alla guerra: oggi tutti sanno che questo grande presidente aveva previsto tutto con molta lungimiranza ed era un interventista in un Paese che non pensava alla guerra.

A riprova di ciò le nostre navi erano state divise in due categorie: quelle sotto sequestro perchè colpevoli di qualche infrazione fiscale e quelle libere.

Ma le predette infrazioni fiscali erano state reperite con tale accanimento e pignoleria (una nave era stata accusata di non aver pagato la tassa di Suez alcuni mesi prima, un'altra del fatto che il suo armatore non aveva pagato il bunker di una nave gemella ad una società inglese) e balzava subito agli occhi che si trattava di un gioco più sottile.

La legge «Affitti e prestiti» americana aveva permesso agli U.S.A. di cedere agli inglesi un centinaio di piccole navi da guerra: una boccata d'aria per gli inglesi in guerra dal 2 Settembre 1939.

Una eventuale cessione agli inglesi delle nostre navi stazionanti nei porti U.S.A. avrebbe significato un altro aiuto notevole per gli inglesi, provati dai durissimi colpi dei sommergibili tedeschi nei primi mesi di guerra (nel 1940 il disavanzo fra affondamenti e nuove costruzioni sarebbe stato per gli inglesi di circa (—) 2.000.000 di tonnellate di stazza). Per di più la nave «Pax Biancamano» avrebbe potuto diventare un magnifico trasporto truppe (proprio in quei mesi gli U.S.A. stavano trasformando nel porto di New York il «Normandie» per adibirlo proprio a trasporto truppe).

Qualcuno dei nostri ufficiali e qualche italiano impiegato a New York in società di navigazione italiane si domandava perchè le nostre Autorità non si muovessero per impedire che le nostre navi cadessero in mani avversarie che le avrebbero adoperate per fare la guerra contro l'Italia: i nostri marittimi pensavano alla dura vita delle loro famiglie in I-[...] scritta dai bollettini di guerra di tutti i contendenti, quindi se qualcosa bisognava fare bisognava farla subito. Infatti lo stato di sequestro non comportava niente altro che un guardiano ad un cartello a piè d'albero, ma fino a quando? E fino a quando gli armatori italiani avrebbero tenuto a bordo l'equipaggio?

Qualcuno della colonia italiana di New York andò a Washington per conferire con l'Ambasciatore Don Ascanio Colonna (che non sembrava molto preoccupato, beato lui) e con l'Amm. Lais, addetto militare che — sapremo poi — era molto addentro alle segrete cose. Dopo un contatto Washington - Roma nel giro di un mese si ebbe la risposta (che vi dirò fra poche righe. Mi sia concessa una parentesi). Ho trovato nel Vol. XVII della storia della Marina Mercantile edita dalla M.Militare una pagina in cui compare il senso di questa risposta durante una seduta segreta avvenuta con il Ministro degli *Esteri* il 16-12-1940: presubilmente cioè dopo il nostro intervento a Washington; a questo punto è lecito porsi una domanda: se non si fossero mossi i nostri marittimi di New York le nostre Autorità sarebbero intervenute?

La risposta inviata da Washington al nostro gruppo di New York era la seguente.

Quando si fossero avverate certe circostanze (e cioè la certezza della requisizione delle navi) sarebbe stato ordinato di danneggiare le navi stesse per il periodo più lungo possibile alle seguenti condizioni: danneggiamenti senza esplosivi, senza incendi, senza pericoli per le persone, senza causare danni al porto e-o alle navi circostanti.

Si trattava di studiare un intervento di alta chirurgia navale, anche se per una volta distruttivo, lasciando intatta la sicurezza in caso di falla, incendio e-o tifone: lasciando cioè intatta la possibilità di dare corrente ai verricelli e ai salpancore per eventuali spostamenti a mezzo rimorchiatore nell'ambito portuale o lungo banchina in maniera autonoma se richiesto dalle circostanze e-o dalle autorità portuali. Severamente vietati affondamenti, incagli e pollution in senso lato.

L'ordine di prepararsi a quanto sopra era immediato, l'ordine di iniziare questo blitz distruttivo - sarebbe arrivato dalla nostra ambasciata di Washington: all'ora «0» tutti dovevano essere pronti.

L'ammiraglio Lais evidentemente sapeva come intercettare l'ordine di sequestro che presto o tardi sarebbe stato emanato dal governo americano a Washington.

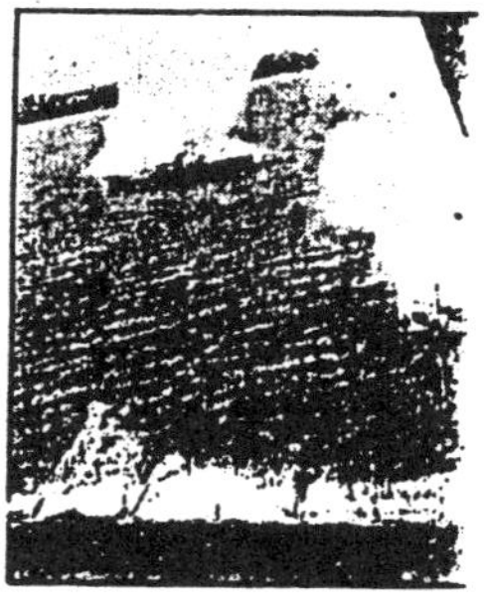

PUNTARENAS (Costarica)

Autoaffondamento in rada (1941) Mn. «FELLA» della Società Italia.

Le navi italiane che si trovavano negli USA al 10/6/1940

ps	ADA	Soc. Nav. Odero
ps	ALBERTA	Italia
p	ANTONIETTA	G. Bozzo Ge
ps	ARSA	Italia
ps	AUSSA	Italia
ps	BELVEDERE	Italia
pc	BRENNERO	Garibaldi
ps	CLARA	Italia
pcis	COLORADO	sa Petroleum Ge
ps	CONFIDENZA	sa Corrado Ge
ps	Conte BIANCAMANO	Lloyd Triestino
ss	DINO	sa Corrado Ge
ss	EURO	Ligure Arm. Ge
ss	GIUAN	G. Gavarone Ge
ss	GUIDONIA	A. Lauro Na
ss	IDA Z.O.	Soc. Nav. Odero
ss	IRCANIA	Garibaldi
ss	LACONIA	sa Tripcovich
ss	LEME	Italia
ss	MAR GLAUCO	Maresca
ss	MONFIORE	Nai Ge
ss	MONGIOIA	Nai Ge
ss	Piero CAMPANELLA	Tito Campanella
ss	SAN GIUSEPPE	Nova Genuis Ge
ss	SANTAROSA	A. Rosasco Ge
ss	S. LEONARDO	Comp. Lig. Nav. Ge
ss	VILLARPEROSA	Comp. Lig. Nav. Ge
ss	VITTORIN	G. Bozzo
m/n	FELLA	Italia
m/n	CELLINA	Italia
m/n	RECCA	Italia

...dnock bldg., San Francisco; Chamber of Commerce bldg., Los Angeles; 1411 Fourth Avenue bldg., Seattle.

APRIL 1, 1941

Is This the Land of Liberty?

When members of the crew of the Italian motorship Leme were loaded into patrol wagons and driven away to the Multnomah county jail declaring that "this was an act of war," a sense of personal outrage no doubt colored their interpretation of the law in the case. Men aroused at dawn and taken to the jailhouse before they have had time to shave, are inclined to jump to the conclusion that the act is illegal. It has always been so. And it would be even more so where the perpetrator of the act was a great big government, with plenty of time on its hands, which might as well wait until the sun was up and coffee over.

We hope, at least, that it was such pique which caused 19-year-old Andrew Tonon to demand, "Is this the United States, where there is liberty and everything?" And which prompted Captain Polonio, with the grease of the sabotage job still on his hands, to gesticulate toward America and shout: "This is inhuman!"

Otherwise—that is, if these outbursts were actual expressions of opinion rather than mere evidences of early morning discomfit—then the WPA teachers and The Oregonian, from which our Italian guests have been learning much of their English, have been doing a poor job of teaching what America is all about. If the outbursts were seriously intended, then somehow our guests have missed the point that law is law in the United States quite as much as in a totalitarian country such as Italy—the difference being that in the democratic case the law is made by duly chosen representatives of the people, whereas in totalitarian states it is created by decree of the dictator.

In the matter of the seizure of 70 Italian, Danish and German ships—in the course of which the seizure of the Leme was an incident—there is such a law, properly passed and ascribed. The governments of Germany and Italy may not approve of it. They might conceivably go to war to prevent enforcement. But the statute providing that our government may assume custody of ships being sabotaged or threatened with sabotage is on the books. And, being on the books, the captain and crew of the Leme have no grounds for complaint. They took refuge in our harbors from unsafe oceans, and under the protection of our flag, they proceeded, with sledge-hammers, emery stones, crowbars and marlinspikes, to obey the orders of their own government and violate the law of our government. Their removal to durance before they could shave was quite legal.

However, that legality does not answer the question of whether it is war. The question of whether it is war must be decided not in the courts of the United States, or by the government of the United States. It will be determined in Berlin and Rome. In view of the general attitude of the United States, our policy of all-out aid, and such incidents as the present one, the axis will have no difficulty in finding an occasion for war if they reach the conclusion that it is time for war. Otherwise, their procedure will be to keep their own people inflamed, and ready for eventualities, but to hold short of a declaration. That is what seems to be indicated now.

Crew Makes Total Wreck Of Italian Ship Machinery

BY LAWRENCE BARBER
Marine Editor, The Oregonian

(See Story on Page 1, Also)

Hardly a machine, motor or instrument aboard the Italian motorship Leme escaped the sledges and wrecking tools of the vessel's crew before she was seized by United States government agencies early Sunday, an inspection of the vessel revealed Monday.

From the anchor winches on the forepeak to the main engines in the bottom of the ship, the crewmen had methodically smashed heavy castings and housings, ripped away electrical wiring and armatures of motors, dropped heavy wrenches and other large steel pieces into cylinders, and scored the cylinder walls with emery dust.

Coast guard officials dared not estimate how long it would take to repair the vessels if such action was desired, but they unofficially admitted that three months as a minimum was a good guess.

Oil Analysis Due

Arrangements were being made for a shore connection with an electrical service for lighting and heating the vessel, and also for making analyses of the oil, water and lubricating oil aboard the vessel before any of it is used, Lieutenant-Commander M. P. Jensen of the coast guard, stated. The coast guardsmen who seized the vessel Sunday noted that the crew members refused to drink their own water, and insisted upon going to the Northwestern grain dock, where the vessel was berthed, for fresh supplies.

Both anchors had been dropped and all chain, estimated at 120 fathoms, or 720 feet, for each anchor, had been played out. The windlasses then had been smashed so the chain could not be raised. Commander Jensen said the windlasses would undoubtedly be among the first machines to be repaired, so the anchors and chain could be returned to the ship. Until then, removal of the vessel to another berth would be very difficult.

Guard Seizes Vessel

Seizure of the vessel was effected by the coast guard, customs service and immigration service, working together, and with the local assistance of the harbor police, Jensen stated.

Coast guardsmen stationed aboard as guards were brought from the Point Adams and Cape Disappointment life saving stations and from the cutter Rose, now being overhauled at Commercial Iron Works shipyard.

Chief Boatswain's Mate Bert K. Cook, in command of the coast guard cutter 265, stationed regularly in Portland, will have custody of the Leme until further orders. The cutter will be tied up alongside the Leme during this period. The Italian crew is being detained at the county jail.

CHE NELLA STORIA DELLA II GUERRA MONDIALE NON EBBE UGUALI

danneggiamento

The Boston Daily Globe

BOSTON, MONDAY MORNING, MARCH 31, 1941—EIGHTEEN

65 Ships Seized in U. S. Ports

WASHINGTON, March 30 (AP)—The government took over all Italian, German and Danish ships immobilized in American territorial waters today—65 vessels in all—after the Naval Intelligence Service uncovered a systematic plot to sabotage the 28 flying the Italian flag.

Officials said 20 of the Italian ships had been quietly "put completely out of business" by their crews. The two German and 35 Danish vessels were taken over along with the Italian ships to guard against similar acts by their crews.

The initial action was taken against the Italian vessels late last night and early today. The Danish ships were being taken over tonight—15 in New York Harbor, eight in Baltimore, three in Boston, two each in Philadelphia, Norfolk and Los Angeles, and one each at Portland, Me., Jacksonville, Fla., and Grays Harbor, Wash. No action was taken against several Danish ships which are in service out of American ports.

(2)

Leme's Flight Plans Doubted

Coast Guard Keeps Watch on Vessel Cited by Libellants; Nothing Amiss.

THE OREGONIAN, THURSDAY, JUNE 19, 1940

Italian Ship Under Guard

U. S. Marshal Fears Flight May Be Tried

Boston Seizures

43 Men Taken From 2 Axis Vessels Here

Movements Of Vessels

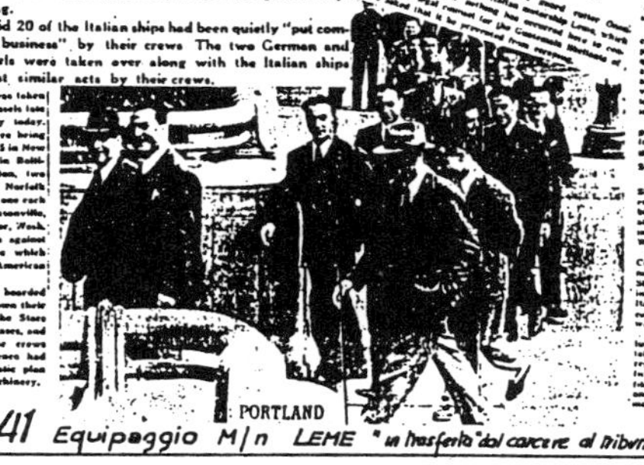
PORTLAND

29.7.41 Equipaggio M/n LEME "in trasferta" dal carcere al tribunale Portland-Oregon

Davanti ai tribunali americani

Vorrei spendere due parole sull'argomento legale: Come si svolse il processo ai nostri marittimi? Quale fu l'accusa? Quale la motivazione della sentenza?

Negli U.S.A. il giudice federale è una carica elettiva quindi una figura fortemente politicizzata.

Questo spiega come negli stati del Sud (Repubblicani) a differenza di quelli del Nord (Democratici) vi furono molte assoluzioni.

Anche la sentenza della Corte di Norfolk (Virginia) (qui a mie mani), rispecchia l'atteggiamento del Sud; comunque sia al Sud che al Nord in definitiva le condanne furono miti (al massimo 3 anni).

Nella realtà dei fatti per prima cosa furono incriminate solo 4 o 5 persone per nave e di questi 4 o 5 solo una persona fu ritenuta responsabile di aver trasmesso l'ordine di danneggiamento agli altri.

Mentre la totalità degli equipaggi fu trasferita in un campo di raccolta i presunti responsabili, condannati a pene variabili da 2 a 3 anni dopo pochi mesi di prigione furono trasferiti nello stesso campo di raccolta degli equipaggi; quindi gli effetti della condanna furono — come dire — eliminati: era ovvio ormai che la guerra era scoppiata e nessuno aveva voglia di perdere tempo e denaro per cause inutili.

Vediamo il meccanismo dell'accusa per la Corte di Norfolk.

La Corte aveva appreso dagli interrogatori che il Cpt. Sagliettto, comandante della «S. Giuseppe» era il più anziano dei comandanti delle navi italiane ancorate a Norfolk ed era stato scelto dall'Ambasciata per essere sistemato in un albergo a terra, quale coordinatore, perchè parlava correttamente l'inglese ed aveva fatto in passato molte soste a Norfolk.

In un secondo tempo un inviato dell'Ammiraglio Lais aveva invitato a pranzo tutti i comandanti su una delle navi e — parlando separatamente con ognuno di loro — aveva spiegato che avrebbero ricevuto tramite Saglietto un telegramma in codice che avrebbe avuto il significato di: DATE INIZIO AL DANNEGGIAMENTO.

Appreso ciò la Corte valutò per prima cosa che il Cpt. Saglietto aveva fatto solo da tramite fra l'Amm. Lais e le navi per la trasmissione di un telegramma (di cui disse di ignorare il significato) e che gli altri comandanti avevano eseguito un ordine: la loro patria era in guerra ed il loro ambasciatore rappresentava di diritto il loro armatore e il loro governo: avendo agito da soli non si trattava di «cospiracy» (associazione a scopo delittuoso, che avrebbe raddoppiato la pena).

Per la seconda cosa la Corte valutò che il danneggiamento aveva reso le navi non autopropellenti nel senso che gli ausiliari di macchina e coperta potevano funzionare e riconobbero che ciò non intaccava la sicurezza; cioè la Corte riconobbe il fatto che le navi all'ancora potevano contrastare qualsiasi evenienza: incendio, falla, spostamento nave, uragano alla pari di tante altre navi americane alla fonda a Norfolk che avevano apparati motori a vapore (che come tutti sanno hanno bisogno di parecchie ore di preparazione per poter partire) o simili a navi che fossero trasportate lungo i moli per grandi riparazioni e quindi non autopropellenti.

Le leggi americane che toccavano questi punti erano state emesse nel 1917 durante la prima guerra mondiale e avevano 2 commi interessanti i predetti argomenti:

Comma II Navi in porto;
Comma III Navi impegnate in commerci con l'estero.

Il Comma III era nato per proteggere le navi da atti che avrebbero potuto danneggiarle non appena uscite dai porti, cosa che in questo caso non si applicava.

Non si poteva altresì dire che i danni arrecati all'apparato propulsivo potessero intaccare la sicurezza dell'equipaggio e del carico (che non c'era) quindi non si poteva parlare di sabotaggio e la Corte applicò il Comma II con un massimo di 2 anni.

Desidero ricordare ancora la coda giallo-spionistica di questa vicenda. Coda che non è di poco conto.

Negli anni '60 due libri di un autore inglese Montgomery Hyde, uno dei quali suffragato da una vistosa presentazione di Antonio Trizzino, tirarono fuori una versione romanzata di quanto ho raccontato. E cioè che l'Amm. Lais, ammaliato da una Mata Hari avente nome di battaglia Cinzia avrebbe ceduto i cifrari della M. Militare italiana, ragion per cui la battaglia di Capo Matapan fu vinta dagli inglesi proprio in base alla conoscenza di detti cifrari.

Io non pretendo di sapere la storia della guerra di spie e la verità nel campo di segreti militari: o se l'Amm. [illegible] a New York fosse [illegible] codici delle navi militari, dico che la lettura dei 2 libri «Il canadese tranquillo» e di «Cynthia» non dimostra nulla di quanto detto sopra, anzi dimostra una scarsa informazione.

Capo Matapan è del 27-28 Marzo 1941 e i libri di Mr. Hyde affermano che la consegna dei codici avvenne qualche settimana dopo il danneggiamento da me raccontato delle nostre navi nei vari porti U.S.A. (29-31 Marzo '41) e comunque dopo la partenza dell'Amm. Lais (tramite una terza persona) dichiarato non gradito il 3 Aprile 1941.

Ci sono stati processi in Italia che hanno dato ragione all'Amm. Lais ma — ripeto — chissà quale è la verità a prescindere dalle persone citate Trizzino incluso.

Chiudo come ho iniziato: non sono né uno storico né un politico: ho saputo di questa storia che non è e non vuole essere una apologia della guerra o del fascismo perchè al massimo si potrebbe parlare di un episodio di resistenza «ante litteram». Ripeto ho saputo di questa storia, ve l'ho raccontata per adornare questa giornata in onore dei marittimi che tanto hanno lavorato e sofferto in tutti i tempi e in tutti i mari e per consegnare ai giovani un ricordo pulito di generosità, di assoluta dedizione, un episodio di alta tradizione marinaresca.

10

Boston Evening Globe

Vol. 206, No. 3 © 1974 Globe Newspaper Co. WEDNESDAY, JULY 3, 1974 Telephone 288-8000 36 Pages

Boston Evening Globe Wednesday, July 3, 1974

INSIDE/OUT

Off Beat

Capt. Carlo Fava had his ship confiscated in Boston by the Coast Guard in 1940 and, for him, it was probably the best thing that ever happened. Page 3.

Friends say goodby to Mrs. K...

He lost a ship but gained a new home and a new life

OFF BEAT

By Douglas S. Crocket
Globe Staff

He's 65 and grey-haired now and one day last week he stood on an Atlantic avenue dock, looked across the harbor toward East Boston, and his mind went back through the years.

"That's where it happened," Capt. Carlo Fava said quietly. "Right over there, the Coast Guard confiscated my ship and interned my crew. It was 34 years ago but it seems like yesterday.

"And it was the best thing that ever happened to me.

"I found a new way of life, a new home, a new country, and a lifetime of opportunity."

But none of that was on Capt. Fava's mind when the United States government boarded his Italian freighter "Dino" on a snowy March Sunday morning more than three decades ago.

"I didn't know what was going to happen to my crew, my ship or anything else," he said. "I was a frightening day. I knew it was coming eventually but I did not realize the impact of the situation until it actually happened."

Capt. Fava, then 31, had sailed his freighter into the Mystic Docks in June 1940 to pick up a cargo of scrap iron.

But the rumbles of World War II were already loud on the European horizon and all foreign vessels in American Harbors were ordered to stay berthed.

And ten days late, Italy entered the war as an ally of Germany.

"Actually the United States was not yet in the war but their allies were involved. And the American government did not know what to do with us.

"So the authorities ordered us to tie up at a pier behind the boiler works in East Boston. And we stayed there for nine months.

"In a way it was pleasant. We were getting our pay from the shipping agent, we could go ashore every night.

"But we could hear the news and read the papers," Capt. Fava said.

"And we knew things were getting worse.

"We watched the 1940 Presidential election. We knew the German submarines were controlling the Atlantic. We knew of the lend lease and the draft. We actually were brought to Faneuil Hall and registered ourselves for the draft as foreign seaman.

"But in February, President Roosevelt signed an order to seize all idle foreign ships and on March 30, the Coast Guard came aboard the Dino and took us into custody.

"They took us to an East Boston immigration detention center, held us there for two months and finally put us on a barred train under border patrol guard. Four days later we ended up in Missoula, Mont. and were quartered in an old CCC camp there," he said.

And it was there, in that camp, that Capt. Fava and 1200 other Italian seamen spent World War II.

"We had our own democracy there," he said. "The authorities were very good to us. And as the progress of the war went in favor of the Americans, they began to parole us to various business firms. the railroad began hiring us at the same rate of pay as their regular employees.

"Our railroad gangs were all over the country and as deputy commander of the camp, I would travel everywhere to inspect their work. And it was then I began to know more about America — began to think about becoming a citizen."

After the war, Capt. Fava found himself working for the Italian shipping lines in Washington, arranging vessel transfers and some for the Marshall plan. And, in time, he won sponsorship from Henry Cabot Lodge and became a citizen of the United States.

And with citizenship papers in hand, Capt. Carlo Fava, the freighter master who had been interned in Boston Harbor, went into the system.

He worked for exporters and importers, and managed New England and North American Italian line offices, bringing cruise ships into northeast harbors.

He ended up as North American assistant manager for the line and in February of this year retired, took his pension, and came back to Boston.

"But I couldn't just sit here. I had to do something," he said.

So last month he opened a Copley Square office and began a business called Sea Air Tours, serving as a general agent for Italian lines running a travel service.

"It's not for the money," he "I have an idea for a new conc travel, combining the best in a sea tours. I don't know if i work but I want to try it."

And so every day, Capt. Fava works in his office in the system which so in him in the early 1940's.

And every once in a goes down to the harbor members. "It was the best ever happened to me," he

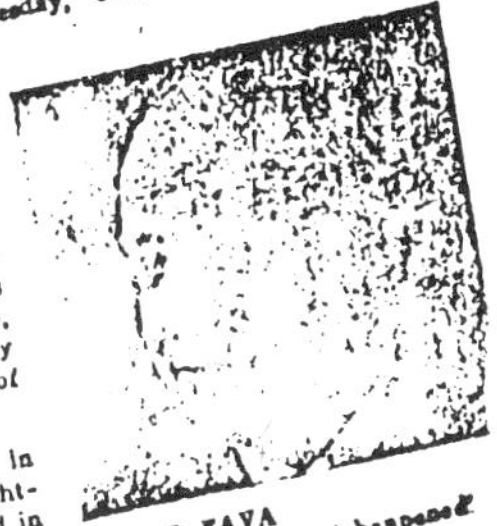

CARLO FAVA . . . 'best thing that happened'

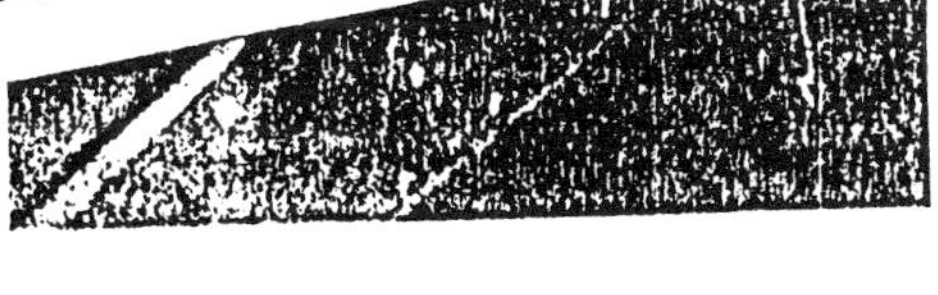

...way Southview Cemetery, four miles south of Atlanta, one of the first graveyards started by Southern blacks after the Civil War.

Soviet censo pulls plug o US networks

Globe Wire Services

NEW YORK — American

...another with champagne amid applause in the Kremlin's St. George Hall.

As the summit broke up, with Mr. Nixon about to fly home and make a televised report to the American people upon arrival in Caribou, Maine, at 7:30 p.m. EDT, Secretary of State Henry A. Kissinger told newsmen he hoped a new strategic arms limitation agreement

This is a view of the beauty of Fort Missoula during 1941-1944. *I Padiglioni,* the linear facade of the building, with an open-space architecture typical of that period of time. The external aspect resembles a University complex to the viewers. In these building lived 1,200 private sailors and New York World's Fair personnel. Although there were many fences all around, the impressive beauty and landscape made it feel like "una Villa," a village rather than a concentration camp, as they were then called; depending on a person's point of view.

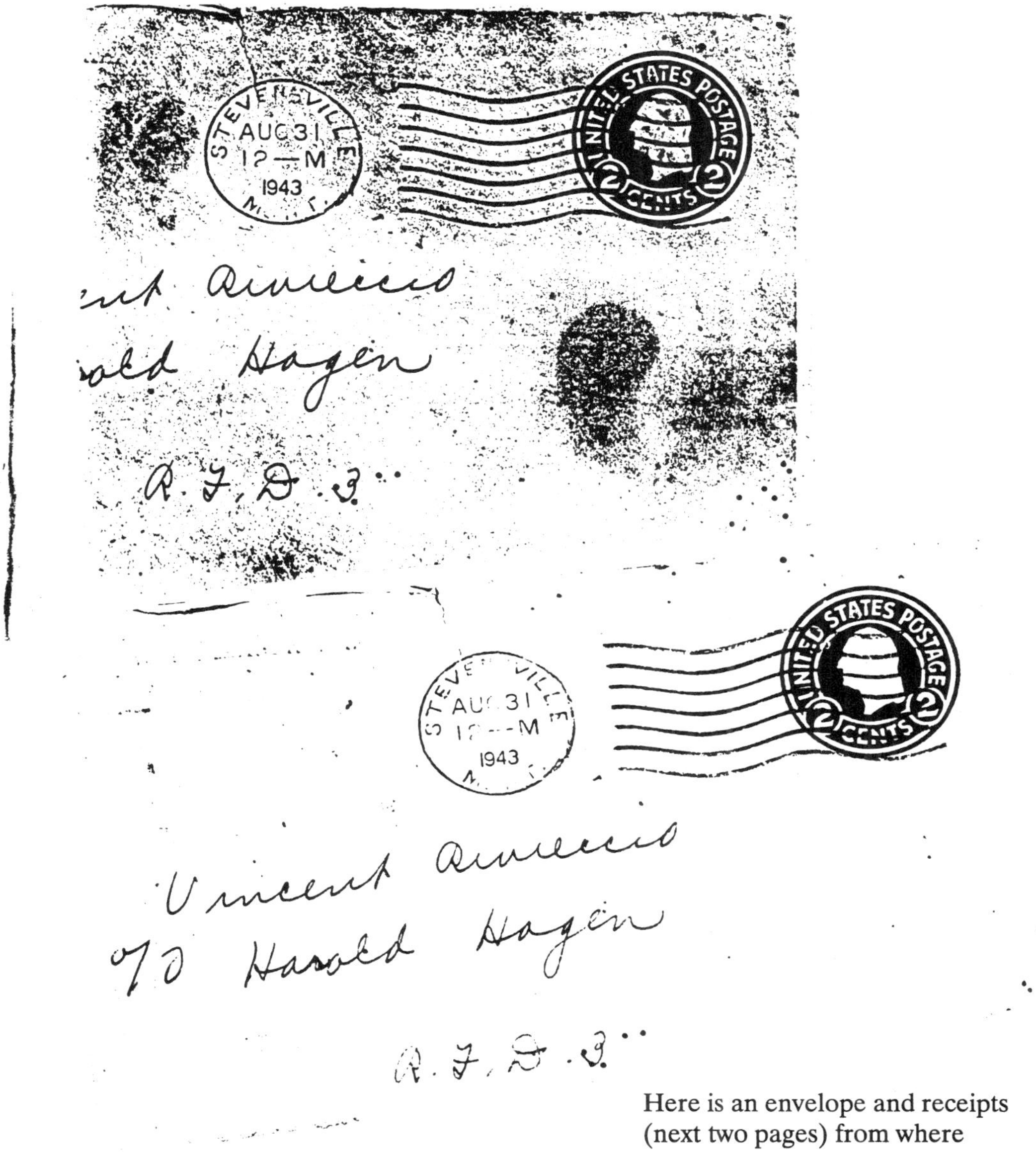
STEVENSVILLE
AUG 31
12 M
1943
UNITED STATES POSTAGE
2 CENTS 2
Vincent Rivieccio
c/o Harold Hagen
R.F.D. 3

Here is an envelope and receipts (next two pages) from where Vincent Rivieccio worked in 1943. One can see the company placed much trust in Rivieccio.

Our Specialty Is Value Not Terms

Stevensville, Mont., _Sept 28_ 194 _5_

M _Vincent Riviccio_

In Account With

Buck Commercial Co.

All Accounts due by 10th of month following date of purchase. . . . 8 per cent carrying charge after due date.
Member of the Credit Exchange

Mdse	63	50
Bal	36	89
	100	39

Our Specialty Is Value Not Terms

Stevensville, Mont., Aug 30 1942

M Vincent Riviccio

In Account With

Buck Commercial Co.

All Accounts due by 10th of month following date of purchase. . . . 8 per cent carrying charge after due date.   Member of the Credit Exchange

	Mdse	36.89
	s/t	3.20
		1.05
		13.07
		14.80
		14.34
		2.90
	october	12.96
		18.72
		17.12
		16.77
		13.21
	Nov	14.33
		0.15
		13.79
		12.90
		11.07
		14.53
		1.77
25481/92		8.85
10 2.		12.29
		254.81

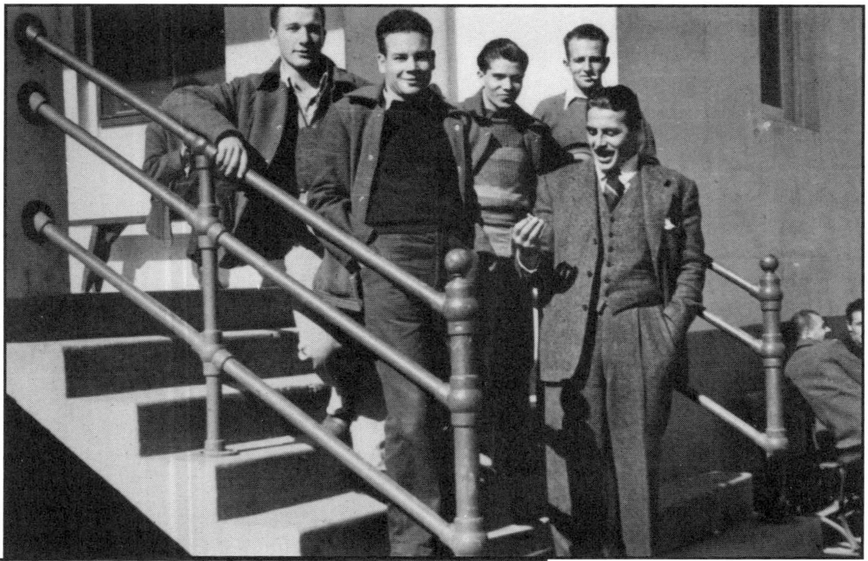

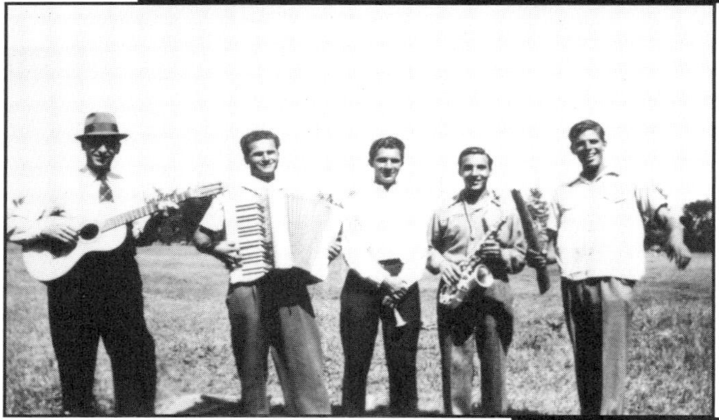

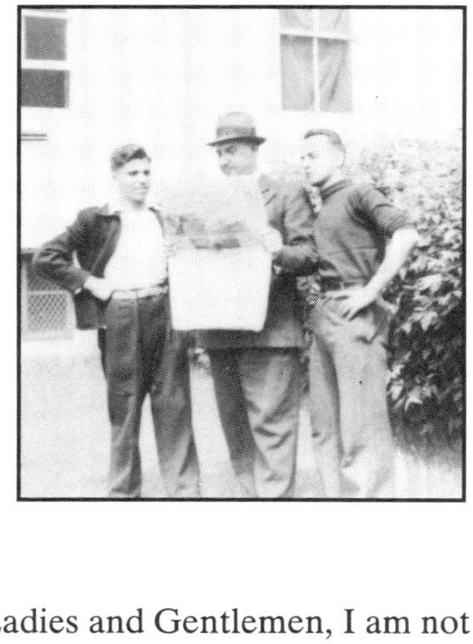

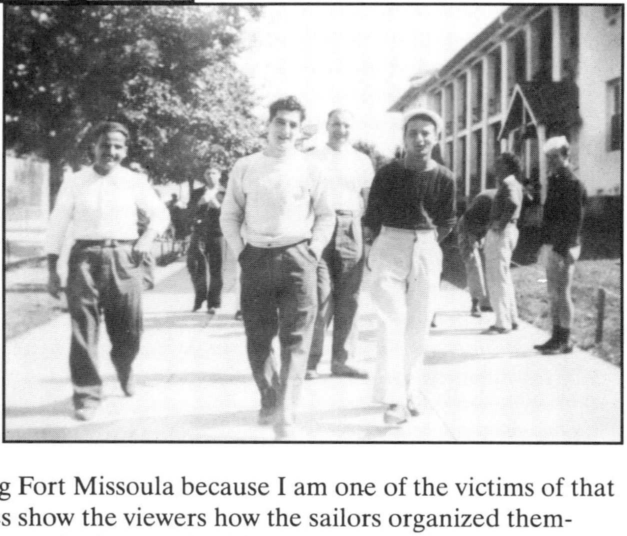

Ladies and Gentlemen, I am not defending Fort Missoula because I am one of the victims of that turbulent time of confusion. These pictures show the viewers how the sailors organized themselves, coming from so far away that they never had seen a land like Montana. In the top picture, he is telling his point of view; middle photo is a musical quintet, bottom right are pedestrians taking a stroll and bottom left the man is reading the news—that was Fort Missoula!

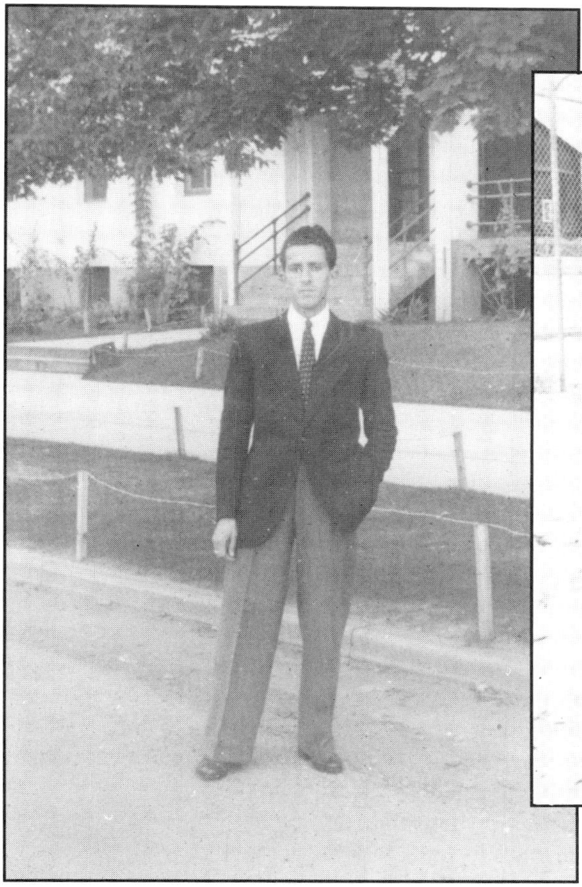

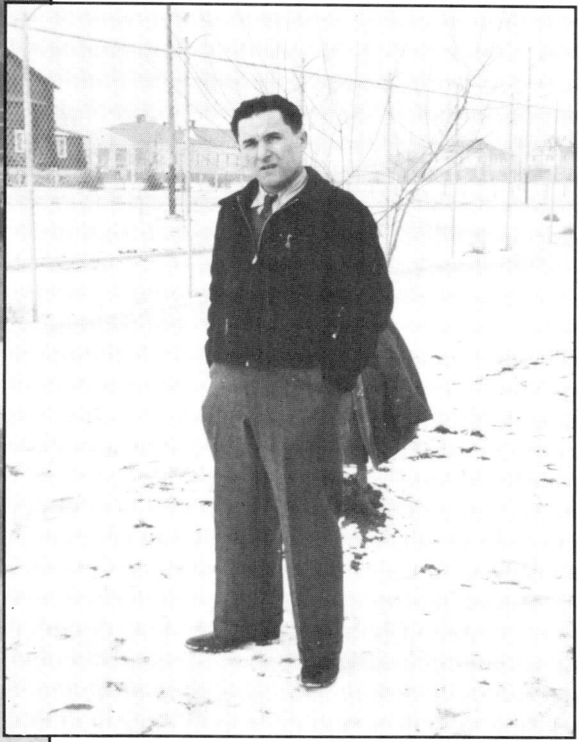

A reminiscence of the past, looking at these two gentlemen. Their elegance and graceful poses, in springtime and in winter. One would think they were in Hollywood rather than in an internment camp! I don't know the names of these men, or if they are still alive. These pictures were taken in 1941-1943.

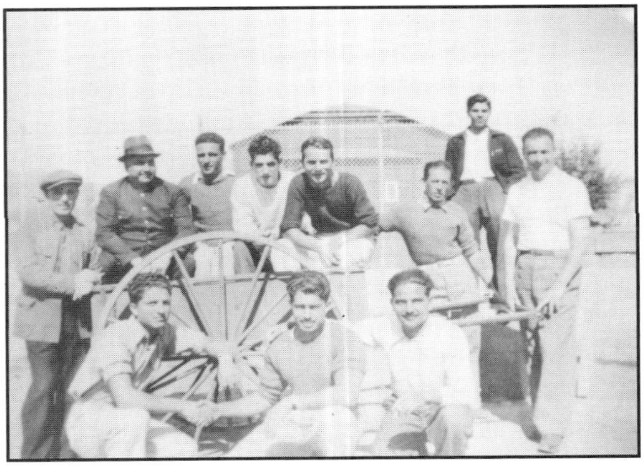

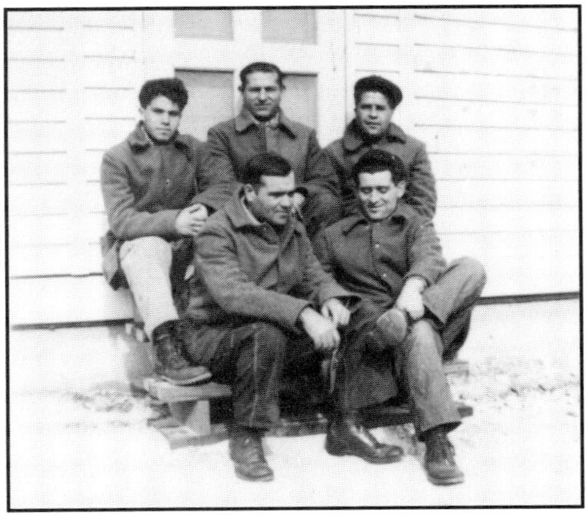

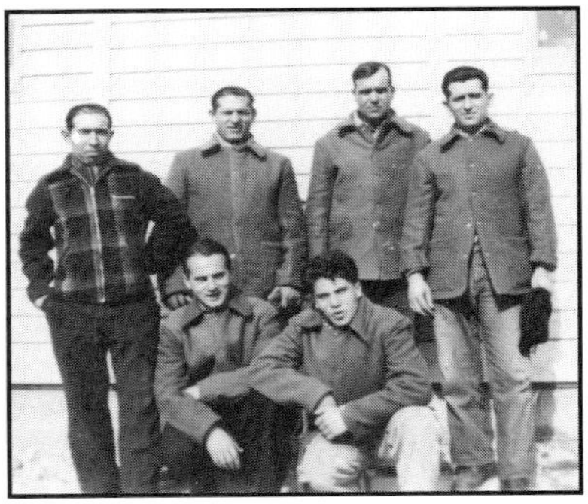

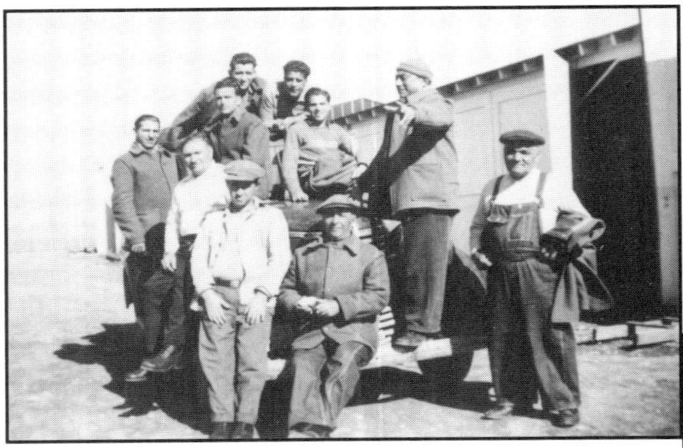

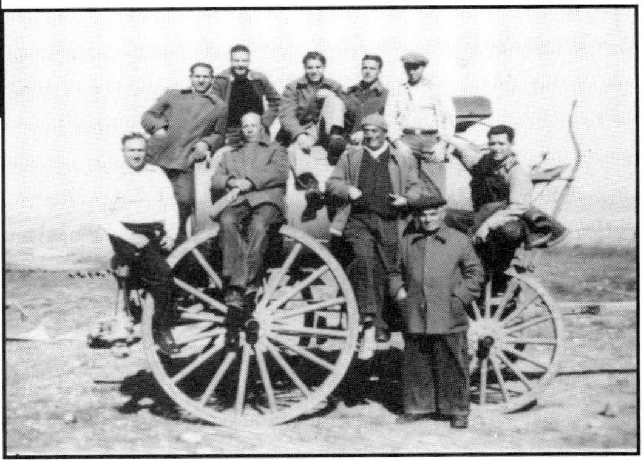

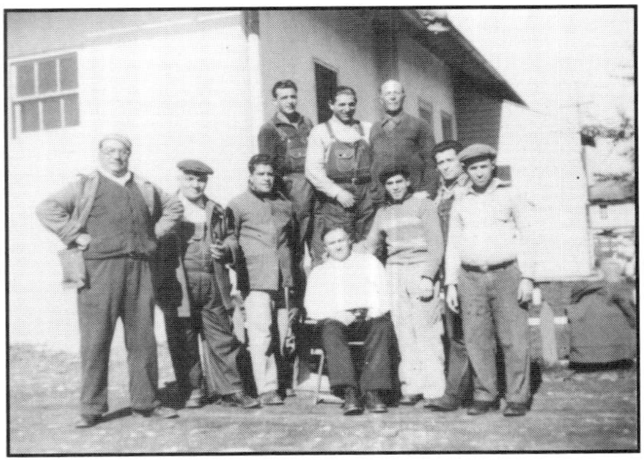

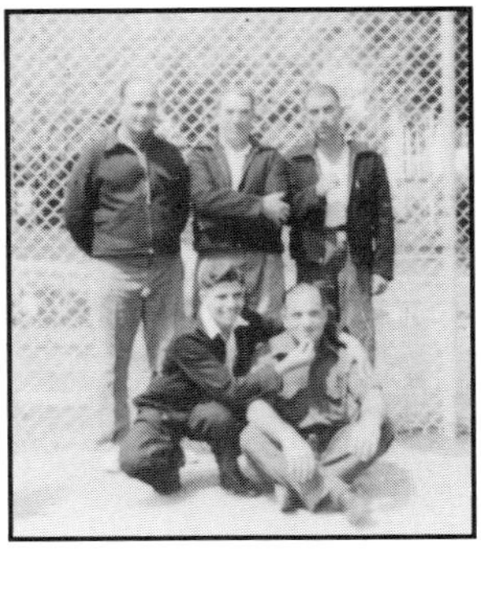

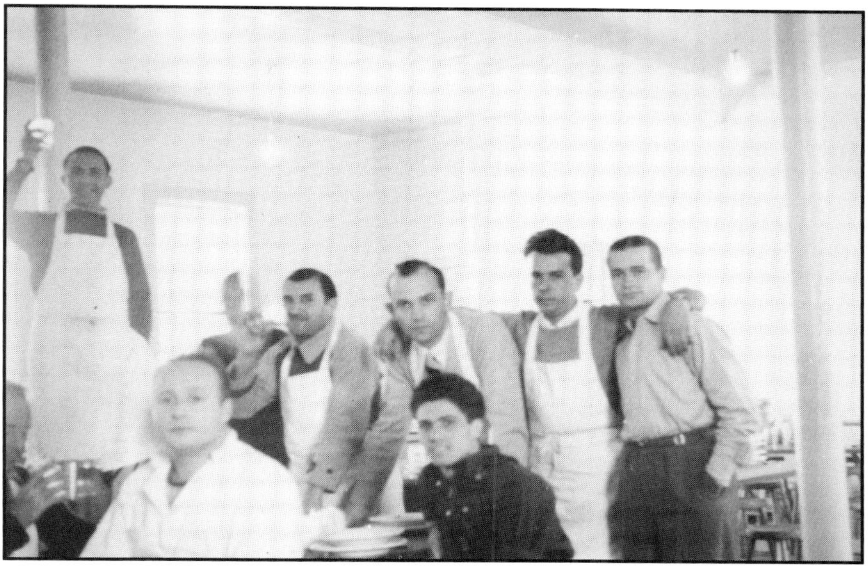

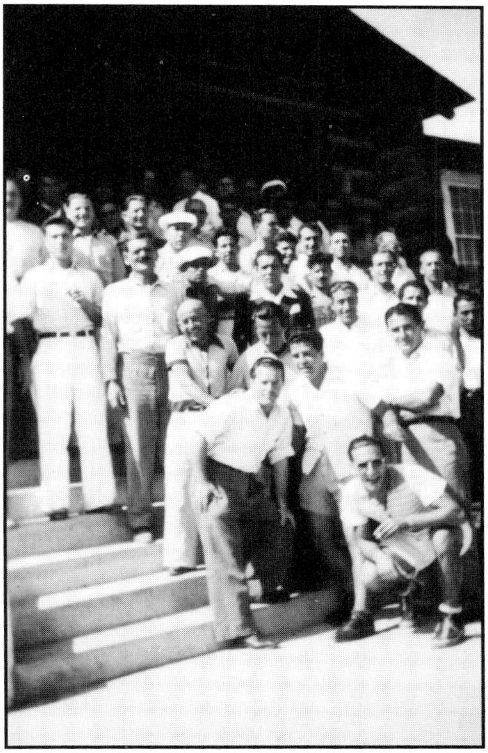

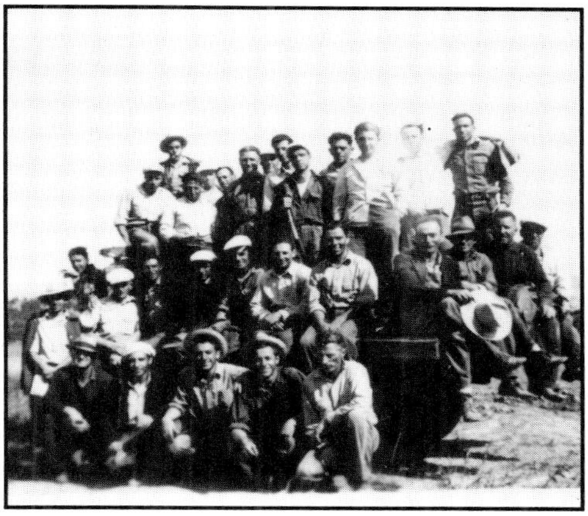

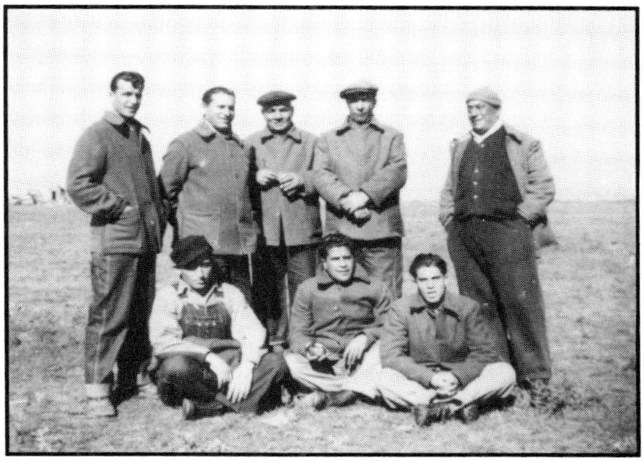

What kind of life do these sailors have? The kitchen, the work parties, the curiosities, the relaxing time, and always, the labor.

Vincent Rivieccio
2527 - 34th Avenue
San Francisco, Calif. 94116-2802

Umberto Benedetti
610 E. Broadway St.
Missoula, Mt. 59802

Caro Amico Umberto,

      mi devi scusare se ti ho fatto aspettare tanto per mandarti queste fotografie (Bianche e Nere) del nostro soggiorno in "Bella Vista"" Fort Missoula, Montana..
Come ben constatare il tempo passa presto e non ci accorgiamo nemmeno.
      Queste fotografie furono prese durante i mesi dell'anno 1941.11!
e in diverse di esse puoi vedere alcune pose del nostro amico Raimondo Visciano, che fu lui il protagonista a farci radunare con voi dopl piu' di 50 anni di assenza da Missoula.
      Noi fummo molto contenti e graditi a vedervi e a passare alcune ricordevoli memorie del nostro passato, ma pero' grazie a Dio dopo aver superato tante difficolta' nella nostra vita durante questo periodo di piu' di mezzo secolo che tali anni son passti come una burrasca temporanea e dobbiamo essere fortunati per arrivare alla nostra eta' radunandoci nel mese di Agosto score e scambiare i nostri sentimenti del passato. Quelle giornate saranno impresse nella nostra memoria sino all'altro mondo.
      Venendo a noi per queste fotografie che ti mando in questo involucro postale ne sono 22 foto in tutto, incluso le due cartoline, una del P/S Conte Biancamano e l'altra della M/V/ Leme, troverai anche foto copie che feci fare da Kinko's e copie che feci io nello stesso locale su macchina regolare. Vedi quale ci piacciano meglio. Le copie le usi e tienele per ricordo, e quando hai finito con le fotografie originali mi farai il piacere di spedirmele di ritorno. Inoltre accludo con tale busta postale le fotografie a colori due ciascune che mi farai la cortesia di darle alla famiglia Cipolato per ricordo del nostro raduno, che loro furono cosi gentili per averci accolti con affezione.

                              Con distinti saluti,
                              Vincent Rivieccio

P.S. Too bad I didn't think to bring all the photos with me when we made the trip to Missoula, we would have avoided uncessary delay. Please don't forget to give my sincerest regards to the entire Alfredo Cipolato family, as you know they are wonderful people and also exent my regards to our friend Mormorato whom we had a brief and cordial visit.

=OVER=

- 2 -

Dear Umberto

Bert (Filiberto) and his gracious wife Marian Apice as well my friend Connie join me in sending you and the Cipolatos as well Mormorato our sincerest regards and many thanks for what every one of did for us while we were there in Missoula.

As far as Lagormarsino is concerned there are 14 by that last name in the San Francisco directory book, If you find out more about this fellow Lagomarsino please let us know and we'll try to trace the family.

Happy Halloween - Happy Thanksgiving from all of us in California, to everyone of you in Missoula.

WRITE SOON

P.S. Too bad I didn't think to bring all the photos with me when we made the trip to Missoula, we would have avoided uncessary delay. Please don't forget to give my sincerest regards to the entire Alfredo Cipolato family, as you know they are wonderful people and also exent my regards to our friend Mormorato whom we had a brief an and cordial visit.

= OVER =

Vincent wrote to me from San Francisco, California, after 54 years absence from Missoula. The family came to see us, as you will see in the pictures on the last pages of this chapter. We had a party in Alfredo Cipolato's backyard. It was a beautiful day in his garden, with trees and flowers in full blossom. We chatted and reminisced, then went to see Fort Missoula and the Museum, and later took a trip to Glacier Park. One of the family members, Filiberto Apice, after returning to San Rafael, California, went on an ocean trip and passed into eternal repose . It seems that destiny played an important role in his life, giving him a chance to see the Fort and his friends in Missoula once more.

CONTE BIANCAMANO
GENOVA

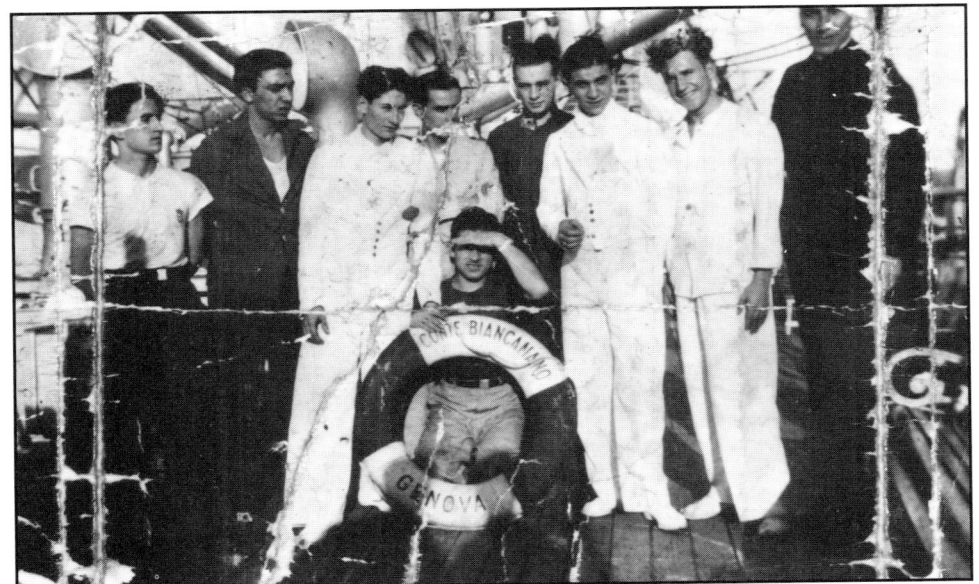

Above: Filiberto Apice is the third from the right, in the white suit. At left, he is the sailor on the right.

Filiberto Apice, at 17, seated on left.

These pictures were taken on the ocean liner *Il Conte Biancamano*. These boys were 17 and 18 years old.

To the Readers:

Believe it or not, sometimes destiny plays an important role in our lives. I am telling the story of one of our friends, Filiberto Apice (the first on the right in the picture). He left Fort Missoula in 1943 or so, and came back in 1995 to visit the Fort and the friends he had left so long ago.

These pictures and others were taken in Alfredo Cipolato's backyard in Missoula. Although these pictures are black and white they still retain the charm of his backyard. We had refreshments prepared by the masterful cooking of Ann Cipolato. We had all sorts of goodies for the guests from California and Florida. We had chit-chat and reminisced about our youth.

However, it seems to me that for Filiberto, destiny played a role. He left Missoula and went back to San Rafael, California. He took an ocean trip as he usually did around Christmastime. His life was spent near boats from his early childhood, and for some unknown reason, he passed away while on this trip. That was his destiny because he loved the ocean, and that was his eternal repose.

This is one of the stories of the boys of the Fort, who, somehow through the love of their spouses and other reasons, chose to stay in the United States until their end. Alleluia.

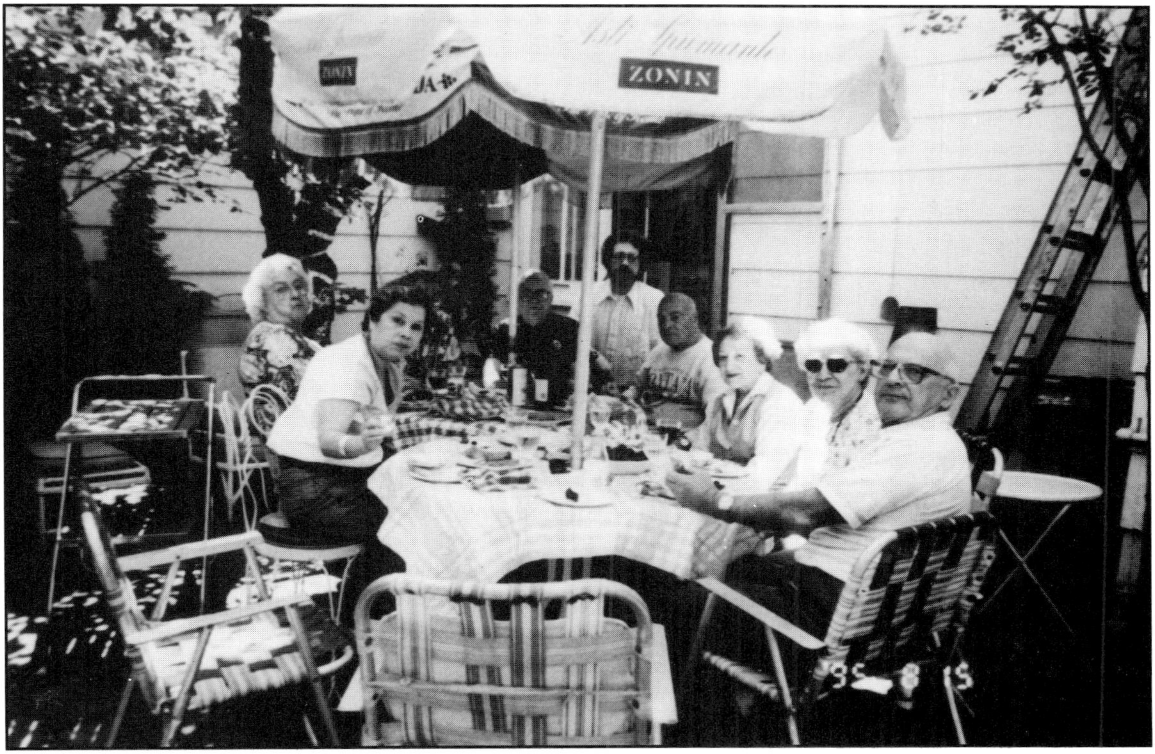
ZONIN
'95 8 15

Right to left: Raimondo Visciano and his wife Lucie, Ann Cipolato, Umberto Benedetti, Alfredo Cipolato's son Denis, Alfredo Cipolato, Filiberto Apico and his wife Mary, and a friend of Riviеccio

Left to right: Alfredo Cipolato, Raimondo Visciano, Umberto Benedetti, Vincent Rivieccio, Filiberto Apice.

About the Author

Umberto Benedetti was born in Vasto, Abruzzo, Italy, and grew up in Genoa, Italy. Mr. Benedetti was employed by Lloyd Triestino in Genoa as an Ebanista and an Assistant Scenographer for the Liner Passenger Boats *Francesco Crispi-Colombo* and *Il Conte Biancamano.*

At the beginning of World War II, he was brought to the United States to Fort Missoula, Montana. He is a veteran of the U.S. Army Corps of Engineers, an Intelligence Researcher, Korea, and is a U.S. citizen.

He worked with the Economic Opportunity Council in the San Francisco Bay area as a community assistant while he was working towards his master's degree in Spanish literature at San Francisco State College. He studied under Luis Cernudo, a Spanish poet from Seville, and Ernest Lombard. Mr. Benedetti attended the University of California at Berkeley. He worked with the Medicare program in cooperation with the Social Security Office. He served as a social worker and taught foreign languages to Peaces Corps volunteers while he was with the E.O.C.

Mr. Benedetti graduates with an Ed.M., the six-year Master's program in Education from the University of Montana, Missoula, on the *Foundations of the Philosophy of Education.* His supervisors were Dr. Robert Anderson, Dr. William Fisher, and John Hunt. He holds a B.A. in Romance Languages from the University of Washington, Seattle, with an emphasis on Spanish Literature and Art. He studied under Garcia Prado and Dr. Anibal Vargas-Baron, poets and writers from Colombia, South America. At the University of Washington, Mr. Benedetti also studied analysis and the criticism of art under Dr. Glen Lutey, chairman of the Department of Philosophy and Fine Arts, and received a certificate. Mr. Benedetti attended Columbia University, New York, studying the aesthetic art and philosophy under supervisor Dr. Maxine Greene, a writer.

He taught Spanish, French and Art at Sacred Heart High School in Miles City, Montana. Mr. Benedetti has published a poetry book, *Montana: Noon A Very Bright Day, Friend*, in 1985. He translated two reports for the State Department about bears, written in Italian; published a book, *The Lifestyle of Italian Internees at Fort Missoula: 1941-1943 (Bella Vista)* in 1986; and published a story, *The Lady and Her Lover*, in 1987, describing the power of love at any age. Included *A Cultural Freedom of the Press* in 1988; a brochure, *Historium*, describing the old Italian language and the name where Italy was cognated for the first time, *Corfino D'Abruzzo*, Italy (1989). Mr. Benedetti participated with a poem, *Come Back to Montana: Where Dreams Begin*, through the National Library of Poetry in 1992, and this book, *The Boys of Fort Missoula, Montana*, in 1997. He retired from the University of Montana, Missoula, in 1985.

> *"Those who cannot remember the past are condemned to repeat it."*
> George Santayana

The National Library of Poetry

11419-10 Cronridge Drive • Post Office Box 704 • Owings Mills, Maryland 21117 • (410) 356-2000

[handwritten: Wonderful "The Sound of Poetry" Select for CB]

October 30, 1992

Umberto Benedetti
610 E Broadway St
Missoula MT 59802

Re: Where Dreams Begin *

This publisher's proof represents your poem as it is now scheduled to appear in print. Please carefully review the publisher's proof . . . check carefully for typographical errors . . . indicate any changes directly on the proof, and return it to us in the enclosed envelope. If your poem is correct as is, please initial the proof, and return it without changes. Please note that you must certify the accuracy of this proof either by making appropriate changes or initialing the proof.

Come Back To Montana

To see the deers and the rivers.
To see the friends deer to you.

To see the mountains the plains and the beauty.
For none more than you are the present and the past.

To see the trees, the rivers and the lakes.
Your loved one of your heart.

Come to see the bucks the lie barren birch groves.
The swiftcurrent-bull head redrock, sherburne lakes.

Come to see the loneliness and security, of the mountains.
The antelope, the goat mountains the elks and calfs deer to you

As the love is to the lovers the teaching is to the teachers.
As the song is to the birds it's here for you! Montana.

I came all the way up here. To light the nostalgic memories.
Of the past remembrances, of my youth.

I came to see the art of nature,
Only in the perfect beauty of the scenery.

I came to see the trees, white wisps of springs
Cling like snow to the branches.

I came back to Montana to see the nature
The happy days of my childhood.
Friend! A grain of wheat cannot bear fruit.
Unless it falls to the ground and dies,
Prompted that merciflul pardon!

—Umberto Benedetti

Please return this proof within four weeks so we can make our scheduled publication date.

* Poems must be 20 lines or less. Only one entry accepted per contestant.

© The National Library of Poetry, 1992

Index

Army Post Hospital—23
Axel, Gertrude H.—14-15
Axis—1

Benedetti, Umberto—48, 54, 124-26
Bitterroot River—36
Boston Harbor—90, 93-94
Brown, Robert—48

Camp Kilmer, New Jersey—86
Carpenter Tools—44-47
Che Bella Vista—1-2
Cipolato, Alfredo—41, 48, 122, 124-25
Cipolato, Ann—124
Cipolato, Denis—124
Civilian Conservation Corps (C.C.C.)—11
Clark Fork River—36
Collaer, N.D.—9

DeLuca, Alexander—9, 37, 86
Detention Camp Regulations—9-10

Ellis Island—1

Fava, Carlo—85, 93
Filiberto, Apice—122-25
Florence Hotel—1
Fort Missoula Barracks—6-7, 23
Fort Missoula Fire Station—5
Fort Missoula Historical Museum—6, 48, 63
Fort Missoula Internment Camp—27
Fort Missoula Mess Hall—28
Fort Missoula, Montana—1-3, 8-9, 17-18, 24, 44, 48, 66-67, 88, 90-91, 93-96, 99, 113, 117
Fort Missoula Recreation Center—11-12
Fort School Books—43
Frazer, Captain Robert—35
Frenchtown, Montana—67

General H.B. Freeman—54-55
Geneva Convention—1
Great Falls, Montana—67, 86
Great Northern Railroad—91

Honorable Discharge—52

Il Conte Biancamano—1, 9, 20, 44, 86, 123
Il Conte Biancamano Orchestra—20-21
Immigration/Naturalization Service—1, 9, 67, 90
Incoronato, Donato Giuseppe—90-93
Incoronato, Jean—91-92
"Italia Bella"—7
Italian Soccer Team—30

Japanese-Americans—1

"La Fiaccola"—37
La Lanterna Di Genova—8

Miles City, Montana—24
Military Police—86
Missoula, Montana—1, 86, 94, 122
Moe, John C.—13-15

Navy Hospital Corps—91
New York World's Fair—67, 88, 113
Northern Pacific Railroad—101-02

Order of Parole—60

Paintings—19
Palace Hotel—1
Panama Canal—1, 44
Paolillo, John Battista—86-87
Pearl Harbor—1
Poem—16
"Prisoners"—29

Raimondo, Lucie—124
Reamer, Robert—11

Rivieccio, Vincent—103, 114-16, 122, 125
Ronzitti, Agostino—88

Saglietto, Capt. Paolo Stefano—86
Sister Agnes (Mary Dooney)—51
Sister Mary Evelyn—61
Sisters of Charity—86
"Springtime in Montana"—25

The White House, Washington, D.C.—62
"Treasure State"—63

University of Montana—48
U.S. Coast Guard—86
U.S. Department of Justice—9

Vasto, Abruzzo, Italy—24
Viola—40
Visciano, Raymond—65-67, 82, 84, 124-25

War Restrictions—89
World War II—1
W.P.A.—11

Ships and Boats:
Alberta—9
Arsa—9
Aussa—9
Brennero—9
G. Locatelli—39
Il Leme—103
Mercy—67
Recca—108
SS Belvedere—67
SS Dino—90, 93
SS Guidonia—86